# new steps in
# religious education
## BOOK 3

### THIRD EDITION

**Michael Keene**

First edition published in 1991.
Second edition published in 1997.
Third edition published in 2002 by:
Nelson Thornes Ltd
Delta Place
27 Bath Road
CHELTENHAM
GL53 7TH
United Kingdom

02 03 04 05 06 / 10 9 8 7 6 5 4 3 2 1

A catalogue record for this book is available from the British Library

First edition ISBN 0-871402-39-5
Second edition ISBN 0-7487-3077-X
Third edition ISBN 0-7487-6459-3

Edited by Melanie Gray
Page make-up by Clare Park

Printed and bound in China by Midas Printing International Ltd.

## Acknowledgements

The author and publishers wish to thank the following for permission to reproduce photographs and other copyright material in this book:

Bridgeman Art Library, London, New York / Bibliothèque Nationale, Paris: Fr 22495 f.235v Combat between the Crusaders and the Saracens in c. 1185, 14th century from Li Romans de Godefroy de Buillon et de Salehadin, 46, / Hermitage, St. Petersburg: Part of a large infantry banner depicting the Last Judgement, Russian, 1695 (silk painted decoration) p 95; Peter Sanders pp 35, 92; Trip pp 60, 61; Trip/J Batten p 106; Trip/A Bloomfield p 94; Trip/T Bognar p 104; Trip/I Genut pp 33, 59, 73, 90, 91; Trip/F Good pp 51, 68 (right), 81, 105; Trip/F Nichols p 62; Trip/C Rennie p 107; Trip/H Rogers pp 53, 63, 66, 74, 76, 78, 79, 80, 85, 93, 97, 99, 100, 101, 103; Trip/Resource Foto p 36 Trip/B Swanson p 67; Trip/B Turner pp 69 (top), 77; Trip/J Wakelin pp 69 (bottom centre), 75.

All other photographs supplied by The Walking Camera.

Every effort has been made to contact copyright holders and the publishers apologise to anyone whose rights have been inadvertently overlooked and will be happy to rectify any errors or omissions.

The scripture quotations (except where specifically indicated in the text) are taken from the Holy Bible, New International Version®. Copyright © 1973, 1978, 1984 by International Bible Society. Used by permission of International Bible Society. 'NIV' and 'New International Version' are trademarks registered in the United States Patent and Trademark office by International Bible Society.

Throughout the series the terms BCE (Before Common Era) and CE (Common Era) are used instead of the more familiar BC and AD. However, in practice, they mean the same thing.

# Contents

# 1 One Church – many churches

## Introduction

If you look under 'Places of worship' in your local *Yellow Pages* you will find a long list of different churches in your area. Look a little closer and you will see that most of the churches can be divided into groups such as:

- Roman Catholic
- Methodist
- Anglican (**Church of England**)
- Orthodox
- Baptist
- Salvation Army.

There are also churches that do not belong to any of these denominations.

### The Christian Churches

Most of the Christian Churches have existed for a long time. Many of them began because people were not satisfied with the Church to which they belonged. They left to form new churches, which developed their own beliefs and ways of worshipping.

The different Churches have many things in common. They share, for example, many basic beliefs. At the same time the differences between them show up in the different ways that each of them worships God. Some, like Roman Catholics and Anglicans, follow set forms of worship that are taken from a prayer book. Others follow a simpler way of worship, which has at its heart hymn-singing and the reading and studying of the **Bible**. Services in most Churches are led by a **priest** or a **minister**. A few Churches, however, do not have either, with members of the congregation taking the services.

### The Christian family

People looking at the Christian Church worldwide often speak of the 'Christian family'. In many ways Christianity is like a family – although it is certainly a big one. There are thought to be more than 20,000 different denominations throughout the world today, with about 1.2 billion Christians meeting regularly to worship. Nine out of every ten Christians belong to one of the four main Churches into which the majority of the different denominations can be grouped:

- The **Roman Catholic Church**
- The **Orthodox Church**
- The **Protestant Church**
- The **Nonconformist Churches**.

# In this unit

## In this unit you will read about the following:

- The Roman Catholic Church which, it is believed, can be traced back to **Peter**, the most important of the disciples of Jesus.

- The Orthodox Church, which is also believed to be a very old form of Christianity. Orthodox buildings are full of important religious symbols.

- The Church of England, the largest Church in England, which is called the **Anglican Church** in other parts of the world.

- The **Baptist Church** and the **Methodist Church**, which are both Nonconformist Churches. The Baptist Church teaches that only adult Christians can be baptised and this makes it different from almost every other Church.

- The **Quakers** and the **Salvation Army**, two important Nonconformist Churches. The Quakers have an almost silent form of worship, while the Salvation Army is well-known for its work among the poorest people.

## In the glossary

Anglican Church
Baptist Church
Bible
Church of England
Methodist Church
Minister
Nonconformist
    Churches
Orthodox Church
Peter
Priest
Protestant Church
Quakers
Roman Catholic
    Church
Salvation Army

# The Roman Catholic Church

More Christians worldwide belong to the Roman Catholic Church than to any other. There are almost 1000 million Catholics throughout the world, with most of them living in South America, North America and parts of Europe.

## Beginnings

Roman Catholics trace the birth of their Church back to Peter, one of Jesus's disciples, whom Jesus called 'the rock'. They believe that Peter became the first **Bishop** of Rome. The **Pope**, the leader of the Roman Catholic Church, is also called the Bishop of Rome. The Pope takes his authority from this link with St Peter. From time to time Roman Catholics believe that the Pope also speaks with God's authority.

**A** There are images of the Virgin Mary in every Roman Catholic church

## Worship

The worship and teaching of the Roman Catholic Church concerns itself with the whole of life from birth to death. It does this through the seven **sacraments**:

- **Baptism**. The Roman Catholic Church baptises babies. It is a serious matter for Catholics if a baby dies before being baptised and the service is carried out as soon as possible after birth. Through baptism the child becomes a member of the Church. Catholics believe that only those who are members of the Church can go to heaven when they die.
- **Holy Communion**. At about seven years of age a child takes his or her first Communion. After this they can take the bread and wine during the **Mass**.
- **Confirmation**. At this service the person being confirmed repeats the promises to lead a Christian life that others made for them when they were baptised.
- Marriage. When they marry, two people promise to love each other and to serve God for the rest of their lives. Because of the belief that children are a gift from God, the Roman Catholic Church does not allow a couple to use any artificial means of birth control (contraception).
- Ordination. Through this sacrament some men offer to serve God and the Church by becoming priests. They take a vow of **celibacy**. Women cannot become priests in the Catholic Church.
- Confession. Catholics confess their sins to God through a priest. They must admit that they are truly sorry for their sins. The priest often asks them to perform a **penance** before he gives them **absolution**.
- Extreme unction. Anointing the sick and the old with holy oil, usually as death approaches, is carried out by a priest. This is done to comfort them.

## The Virgin Mary

The **Virgin Mary** plays a very important part in Roman Catholic worship. Mary was the mother of Jesus. Catholics believe that, because she was without sin, at the end of her life Mary was taken directly into heaven without dying. There are statues of Mary in every Roman Catholic church. Catholics believe that she prays for them in heaven and many prayers in services are directed to her.

**B** The stoup just inside a Roman Catholic church holds the holy water

### In the glossary

| | |
|---|---|
| Absolution | Mass |
| Baptism | Penance |
| Bishop | Pope |
| Celibacy | Sacraments |
| Confirmation | Virgin Mary |
| Holy Communion | |

 **Find the answers**

- Who is the head of the Roman Catholic Church and from whom is he thought to be descended?

- How many sacraments are there?

- Which saint do Roman Catholics believe can help them with their prayers?

**Learning about, learning from**

1 Write one-sentence answers for each of the following questions.
   a. What happens at confirmation?
   b. Why do you think people being confirmed repeat the promises made for them at baptism?

2 Roman Catholics often ask Mary or one of the saints to pray for them.
   a. When two people have an argument, it often helps for someone who is not involved to try to sort things out. Why do you think this often helps?
   b. Why do Catholics often ask Mary to pray for them?
   c. Why do some Catholics find it helpful to pray in front of a statue of the Virgin Mary?

 **Extra activity**

The Roman Catholic Church claims it is the original Christian Church from which the other Churches have broken away. Why do you think Roman Catholics believe this is very important?

# The Orthodox Church

The Orthodox Church is a family of Churches rather than one single Church. Like the Roman Catholic Church it, too, claims to be the oldest form of Christianity, going all the way back to the time of Jesus. In the Great Split of 1054 the Orthodox Church broke away from the Roman Catholic Church and it has been a separate Church ever since. Today more than 120 million people belong to the Orthodox Church in eastern Europe, Russia and the eastern Mediterranean.

## Two groups

For centuries the Orthodox Church has been made up of two main groups:

- The Eastern Orthodox Church, which includes the Russian, Serbian and Greek Orthodox Churches. Around 80 per cent of all Orthodox Christians belong to the Eastern Orthodox Church.
- The Oriental Orthodox Church, which is the older of the two groups, has five member Churches. They include the Armenian and Coptic Churches.

## Orthodox buildings

Orthodox church buildings express what their worshippers believe about God and the universe in which they live. They are full of symbols to help worshippers

**B** The iconostasis is a screen separating worshippers from the altar

understand God. All churches are square and topped with a dome. Standing within the square the worshipper thinks of God ruling over the four corners of the earth. In addition:

- the floor represents the earth
- the richly decorated ceiling represents the heavens
- the circle of the dome represents the eternal nature of God – a circle does not have a beginning or an end.

## Orthodox worship

Each Orthodox Church has its own language and customs, but all of the Orthodox Churches have a great deal in common with each other. Their services are very colourful, and the clothes (vestments) worn by the priests are beautiful and richly decorated. The smell of incense fills the air as the priest chants the words of the services, to be met in response by the choir and congregation.

There are many **icons** in the church. These are special paintings or mosaics of religious people such as Jesus, the Virgin Mary or one of the saints. Before a service begins, people often bow before an icon and kiss it.

**A** The priest in an Orthodox church is responsible for leading the very important service of the Divine Liturgy

Sometimes an icon is surrounded by burning candles, which members of the congregation have lit as they offer a prayer to God. A screen separates the **altar** from the people. This is called the **iconostasis** and is covered with icons.

Every **Sunday**, and on festival days, Orthodox Christians celebrate their most important act of worship – the **Divine Liturgy**. During this service the priest carries the bread and wine to the altar. The people can just see the priest through the iconostasis as he offers them to God. The doors in the iconostasis (the Royal Doors) are then opened as the priest brings the bread and wine through to give to the people. In other Churches this service is called Holy Communion.

C Icons are special religious paintings that Orthodox Christians use in their worship

## In the glossary

| Altar | Iconostasis |
| Divine Liturgy | Sunday |
| Icons | |

## Find the answers

- When did the Roman Catholic and Orthodox Churches separate?
- What is the Orthodox service of Holy Communion called?
- What is an icon?

## Learning about, learning from

1 Study picture C.
  a. Write down three things you notice from the photograph.
  b. List three ways in which an Orthodox church is different from other churches. In this book you will find photographs of other churches to help you.

2 a. Which two main Churches make up the Orthodox Church?
  b. Give two examples of Churches within each of the main groups.

3 Take two symbols in an Orthodox church and explain what they mean.

## Extra activity

In Orthodox churches the altar is behind a screen. It is here that the bread and wine are prepared for the Divine Liturgy. The altar is the place where God is found. The people can just glimpse the priest. What is the deep spiritual truth here?

# The Anglican Church

The Church of England was formed in the sixteenth century and it is the most important Church in England. The Queen is the head of the Church. The Church plays a leading part in the national life of the English population. For example, some of its bishops belong to the House of Lords – a privilege offered to no other Church.

When churches following the teachings of the Church of England were set up in other countries of the world, they became part of the Anglican Church. The Church of England is part of the Anglican Church. The Anglican Church is particularly strong in Australia, Canada and the West Indies, with many followers also in South America. There are about 70 million Anglicans in the world today.

## Two kinds of Anglicans

Although the Anglican Church is one Church, it does contain Christians who hold many different points of view. In particular, two groups exist side by side:

- 'High Church' Anglicans. These are Anglicans who have similar beliefs and ways of worshipping to Roman Catholics. They use incense and candles in their services. They bow before the altar as they enter and leave church. They go to **confession** to seek forgiveness for their sins. In their churches the service of Holy Communion is often called the Mass.
- 'Low Church' Anglicans. The members of this group are also called Evangelicals. These Anglicans are much closer to the Nonconformist Churches, such as the Baptists and Methodists, in their beliefs and ways of worshipping. They emphasise the importance of the Bible and the need to follow its teachings in the Christian life.

All Church of England churches use services from a prayer book. In 2001 a new prayer book, *Common Worship*, was introduced. This means there are certain common ingredients that are found in Anglican services wherever they are held:

- Hymns.
- Psalms.
- Set prayers.
- Bible readings. Most Anglican services include three Bible readings – one from the **Old Testament**, one from the **Gospels** and one from the letters found in the **New Testament**.
- The **sermon**.

A The service of Holy Communion in an Anglican church is conducted from the altar

### In the glossary

| | |
|---|---|
| Confession | Old Testament |
| Gospels | Sermon |
| New Testament | |

B A service in an Anglican church

C Inside an Anglican church

## Find the answers

- What is the Anglican Church?
- Who is the head of the Church of England?
- What do most Anglican services contain?

## Learning about, learning from

1 In picture C you can see the inside of a Church of England church. Write down five things you notice about it.

2 What is the difference between the Anglican Church and the Church of England?

3 What are the main differences between 'High Church' and 'Low Church' Anglicans?

4 Do you think it is important for the Church of England to play an important part in the life of English people? Explain your answer.

## Extra activity

Although no more than 5 per cent of the population of England go to church regularly, over 50 per cent have their children baptised, marry and are buried with a Church of England service. Do you think this should be permitted? Should these important services be reserved for those people who attend church regularly? What are the main arguments for and against?

# The Baptist and Methodist Churches

The Churches in England that do not belong to the Roman Catholic, Orthodox or Anglican Churches are called Nonconformist Churches. This is because they do not conform to (follow) the teachings of the Church of England. The two most important Nonconformist Churches are the Baptist Church and the Methodist Church.

## The Baptist Church

The Baptist Church began at the beginning of the seventeenth century when a group of people belonging to the Church of England left the country because they were being persecuted. They were suffering because they did not believe the Church's teaching that only babies should be baptised. They believed that only adults who believed in Jesus as their Saviour should be baptised. They started a Baptist Church in Amsterdam.

**A** The service of Holy Communion, called the Breaking of Bread, is held in a Baptist church

Soon some Baptist believers returned to England and set up a Baptist church there. Since then, Baptists have spread all around the world. The Church is particularly strong in the USA. Although it agrees with other Churches on most things, it still teaches that only adults can be baptised. We will look at this service, known as **believer's baptism**, on pages 44 and 45.

## The Methodist Church

While John Wesley and his brother Charles were at Oxford University in the early eighteenth century, they formed a group that encouraged its members to read the Bible and pray 'methodically'. On leaving university John Wesley became a Church of England clergyman, but his preaching soon frightened the Church authorities. In 1738 he was forced to hold his religious meetings in the open air and great crowds gathered to hear him speak. It is said that during his lifetime Wesley travelled more than 400,000 kilometres on horseback to preach in different places. Often his first meeting of the day was at 4 a.m., with several more to come before the day ended. Crowds of 20,000 people or more often gathered to hear him preach as dawn broke.

Although Wesley remained a member of the Anglican Church, he also began to build churches for his followers to worship in. He ordained his own ministers and organised his followers into 'class-meetings' so they could be taught. By the time of his death in 1791 there were 70,000 members of the Methodist Church and 300 full-time ministers to look after them.

Methodists today follow the same principles that John Wesley introduced. The services of the Anglican Church at the time were dull and lifeless. Wesley placed a great emphasis on singing hymns. His brother Charles wrote some of the best-known hymns and many of these are still sung today. Wesley also introduced open prayers, Bible readings and the sermon, which are still important features of Methodist worship today.

**B** The Methodist Church is a Nonconformist Church

## In the glossary

Believer's baptism

 **Find the answers**

- What are the Nonconformist Churches?

- What makes the Baptist Church different from most other Churches?

- Which Methodist wrote many hymns, some of which are still sung today?

 **Learning about, learning from**

1 Each of the following statements is either true or false. If true, copy it into your exercise book or file. If false, write down a correct version.
   a. Baptists believe that only babies should be baptised.
   b. Believer's baptism is an important service in the Methodist Church.
   c. The founder of the Methodist Church was Charles Wesley and many of the hymns sung by Methodists were written by John Wesley.
   d. The Methodist Church took its name from the 'methodical' way that Wesley and others studied the Bible when they were at university.
   e. By the time of John Wesley's death there were 7000 members and 3000 ministers in the Methodist Church.

2 Study picture B.
   a. Write down three things you notice about this Methodist church.
   b. Compare this Methodist church with either an Orthodox church (page 8) or a Church of England church (page 11). Write down two differences you notice.

## Extra activity

Baptism shows that a person has become a member of the Christian Church. Why do Baptists believe that only adults, and not babies, should be baptised?

# The Quakers and the Salvation Army

The Quakers and the Salvation Army are two other important Nonconformist denominations. In their own way both of them are rather different from other Churches.

## The Quakers

In 1652 the Society of Friends was started by George Fox. Shortly afterwards, members became known as Quakers when Fox told a judge that he should 'quake' in the presence of God. From the beginning Fox told his followers that they should never take an oath (a promise in a court of law) on the Bible because the truth is far more important than any book. Christianity was a matter of following 'the light within' rather than any religious rules.

Quakers have always been pacifists. This means they do not believe in going to war or using violence in any situation. During the First and Second World Wars, for example, Quakers took up non-combative (non-fighting) roles such as driving ambulances and stretcher-bearing.

## Quaker worship

Quakers meet together for worship in simple buildings called **meeting houses**. Inside, seats are gathered around a central table which holds little more than flowers. The service continues largely in silence and this is broken only when someone feels prompted by the **Holy Spirit** to speak. If no one speaks, the Holy Spirit is speaking to people in the silence of their hearts. Quakers do not celebrate Holy Communion or any of the other sacraments.

## The Salvation Army

The Salvation Army was founded by William Booth in 1878. He wanted to help poor people, many of whom had never been involved in church worship. From the start, the organisation was run like an army, with its leaders holding such positions as general, colonel and lieutenant. It is still organised in the same way today. Within a few years of starting, the Salvation Army had begun the social work, at home and overseas, for which it is so well-known today.

Each local Salvation Army corps meets in a **citadel**, which it uses as a base to reach out into the local community. Worship is usually led by a brass band and includes much hand-clapping and the shaking of tambourines. Like the Quakers, the Salvation Army does not celebrate any of the sacraments. Various social activities are run from the citadel. Most of the Salvation Army's work is in cities and

**A** A Quaker service is largely one of silence

towns, and includes running soup kitchens, working with the homeless and tracing missing people.

The Salvation Army now has workers in over 100 countries. When there is a national disaster, such as a flood or an earthquake, the Salvation Army is among the first to offer help. They believe that by doing so they are showing the love of God in action.

**In the glossary**

Citadel          Meeting houses
Holy Spirit

## Learning about, learning from

1 Write down three ways in which Quaker and Salvation Army worship differ, and one way in which they are similar.

2 Members of the Salvation Army spend much time working among the poor and needy. Why do they see this as an important part of being a Christian community? Read Matthew 25.27–40 before answering this question.

3 Silence is at the heart of Quaker worship.
   a. What do Quakers hope to hear by sitting in silence in their services?
   b. Have you ever tried to remain silent for a period of time? Did you find it easy? What made it difficult?
   c. How do you think you might benefit from having a silent time each week?

**B** The service in a Salvation Army citadel is usally led by a brass band

## Find the answers

- Why were the Quakers given their name?

- Why was the Salvation Army begun by William Booth in the nineteenth century?

- What are the names of the buildings in which Quakers and members of the Salvation Army meet for worship?

## Extra activity

Quakers believe God speaks to them in the silence of their own hearts. Do you ever hear your conscience speaking to you? What kind of things does it say to you? Do you think it is the 'voice of God'?

# 2 God and the gods

## Introduction

Most of the world's great religions began with the life and teachings of a man who gathered a group of disciples (followers) around him. After the teacher's death, these followers dedicated themselves to the spread of the teacher's message. Much of that message centred on God and the demands He made.

Although some religions, such as Hinduism and Judaism, appear to be very old, they belong to a recent chapter in human history. Hinduism, for example, began about 6000 years ago, but long before that men and women were worshipping powers which they believed to be greater than themselves. In these early religions, however, people rarely believed in one supreme being. They were more likely to believe in many powerful spirits or gods who controlled different parts of their lives. These gods were thought to be everywhere in nature – in trees, mountains, rivers and stones.

Two fears dominated the lives of ancient peoples and these were reflected in their religious beliefs:

- The fear of death. People were certain that the spirits of their dead ancestors could return to haunt them and so they worshipped them. Death was the great unknown and was, therefore, frightening.
- The fear of nature. Natural events, such as a flash of lightning across the sky, torrential rain or a hurricane, were all thought to be signs that the gods were angry. The spirits (gods) needed to be kept happy and so were worshipped. Each god was seen as having control over some part of nature, although one god was often given more authority than the others.

### Monotheism

Around 2000 BCE, during the time of the early ancestors of the Jews, the worship of many gods or spirits was still common. The Jewish scriptures speak of **Abraham**, who came firmly to believe that there was one God, not many. This God made the world and the whole universe. He was the God of unlimited power. At the same time a power of darkness and evil waged a constant battle against the one God.

This belief in the one God is called monotheism. Judaism, Christianity, Islam, Hinduism and Sikhism are all monotheistic religions. They teach that the world could know nothing about God unless God had chosen to reveal himself. He did this through a few chosen, and very special, human beings. Buddhism is different to the other religions. Buddhists do not believe in God.

# In this unit

## In this unit you will read about the following:

- The Christian **Trinity**. Christians believe in the one God who can be experienced, or known, in three different ways – as God the Father, God the Son and God the Holy Spirit.

- The Jewish God. Jews worship the God who, they believe, made all that exists in and beyond the universe.

- The Muslim God, **Allah**. Allah demands that all his followers submit themselves to His will. This will is laid down in the **Qur'an**.

- The Hindu God, **Brahman**. In Hinduism Brahman is the God over all other gods.

- The Sikh God, **Nam**. Sikhs believe it was God who made the world, but He cannot take on any human form. Sikhs try to keep God's name in their minds at all times.

## From the *Epic of Gilgamesh*

The *Epic of Gilgamesh* is a famous ancient Babylonian poem. In it the hero says to a goddess:
*O let me not see the death I constantly fear.*
The goddess replies:
*Gilgamesh, where are you wandering to? You will not find the life you seek. When the gods made mankind, they set death aside for mankind but they kept life in their own hands.*

## In the glossary

| | |
|---|---|
| Abraham | Nam |
| Allah | Qur'an |
| Brahman | Trinity |

# The Christian Trinity

Christians believe there is one God. God is so great that no human being can understand him fully. God can be known, or experienced, in three different ways. This belief is called the Trinity. God can be known as:

- God the Father. God the Father made the world and everything that is in it. Nothing is beyond the power of God the Father.
- God the Son. God came into the world as Jesus Christ in first century Palestine. Christians speak of Jesus as their Saviour, Friend and Lord. He showed the people how they should live by setting them a perfect example. At the end of his life he died for the sins of the whole world. Three days later God the Father brought Jesus back to life.
- God the Holy Spirit. Jesus promised his disciples that, after he had left the earth, he would send his Holy Spirit to them. The Holy Spirit would enter their hearts and minds. Christians believe that God's power and love are at work in the world today through the Holy Spirit. The Holy Spirit is usually pictured as a dove, the bringer of peace. The Holy Spirit brings guidance, comfort and help to individual Christians and to the Church as a whole.

It is important to understand that Christians do not believe in three gods. The quotation in the box on the next page makes this clear. This **Creed** is still repeated as part of many Christian acts of worship. It shows that Christians believe that God the Father, God the Son and God the Holy Spirit are three separate beings and yet united in the one Godhead. How this can be true is a mystery that no one can begin to understand.

## God as love and as the judge

Two sides to God come out of the Bible:

- God as love. Christians stress that God loves the world. This love is at the heart of the story of Jesus, which is told in the four Gospels of the New Testament. Through the life and death of Jesus, God is able to forgive the sins of the human race. This is the message that the Christian Church has preached for over 2000 years.

**A** The dove is a popular symbol for God the Holy Spirit

• God as the judge. The Bible also speaks of God as the judge. Christians believe that, at the end of time, all men and women will appear before God to be judged on the lives they have led. The good will enjoy heaven for all time, while the wicked will be sent to hell. Only God, in his great wisdom, could possibly decide who will end up where.

**B** The belief of this group of Christians is based on a belief in the Trinity

# The Nicene Creed

The Nicene Creed is a very early statement of Christian belief. It said this about the Trinity:
*We believe in one God, the Father, the almighty, maker of heaven and earth, and of all that is seen and unseen... We believe in one Lord, Jesus Christ, the only Son of God... We believe in the Holy Spirit, the lord, the giver of life.*

### In the glossary
Creed

 **Find the answers**

• Who do Christians believe made the heavens and earth?

• Who do Christians believe came into the world as a human being?

• Who, according to Christians, is God's power and love in the world today?

**Learning about, learning from**

1 Read the extract from the Nicene Creed in the box.
   a. Rewrite the extract in your own words.
   b. What does it tell you about the beliefs that Christians hold about the Trinity?
   c. What do you think the word 'almighty' means?
   d. What do you think the phrase 'giver of life' means when it used about God the Father and the Holy Spirit?

2 Christians often say they cannot see God the Holy Spirit but they can feel His presence in the world. What might they have in mind when they say this?

 **Extra activity**

Can you think of a symbol that could be taken from everyday life to help Christians understand the Trinity (three things in one) a little better?

# The Jewish God

**A** Every Jew recognises that there is one God

For Jews there is only one God, an all-powerful being who created the world and chose the Jews to be His special people.

## A God of action

The Jewish scriptures open with an account of God creating the world. The universe was formless until God's Spirit began to breathe life into it. He created everything from the sun, moon and stars down to the tiniest forms of life. Finally, He created the first man and woman. All this took God six days before He rested on the seventh day. Jewish people remember this each week as they celebrate the **Sabbath Day**, the day on which all work stops.

Jews believe they were chosen by God to be His special people. God entered into an agreement with Abraham, which promised that God would give the Jewish people a country of their own – **Israel**. In return, they were expected to keep God's laws, especially the **Ten Commandments**. The **prophets** told them this meant that they must:

• treat each other justly and fairly
• live wisely and faithfully before God.

Jews believe this agreement with God still exists today.

About 4000 years ago the Jews became slaves in Egypt. They were there for over 400 years until God sent them a new leader, **Moses**. He took them across a sea that miraculously opened up before them to their new home. This journey is known as the **Exodus** and is celebrated each year by Jews everywhere in the **Passover** festival.

## No statues

Everything that Jews believe about God comes from these early experiences. They learned that God cannot be represented by any statue or image. You can read what the second of the Ten Commandments told Jews about this in the box on the next page. The decorations in a **synagogue** are simply letters of the Hebrew alphabet because no pictures are permitted.

Throughout their long, and often painful, history Jews have believed that their God is not simply one among many gods. Their God stands alone. He cannot be compared with the gods of any other faith. This is how this God is described in the Jewish scriptures:

> Not to us, O Lord, but to your name be the glory, because of your love and faithfulness... their idols are silver and gold... They have mouths, but cannot speak... May you be blessed by the Lord, the Maker of Heaven and Earth. The highest heavens belong to the Lord, but the earth has been given to man.

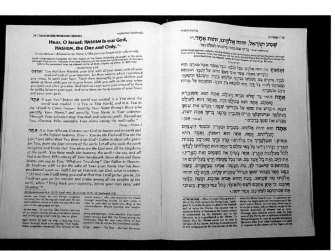

**B** The Shema is the most important statement of Jewish belief – a belief in the oneness of God

# The Ten Commandments

The second of the Ten Commandments strongly condemns any attempt to make a likeness of God:

*You shall not make for yourself an idol in the form of anything in Heaven above or on the Earth beneath... You shall not bow down to them or worship them.*

## In the glossary

| | |
|---|---|
| Exodus | Prophets |
| Israel | Sabbath Day |
| Moses | Synagogue |
| Passover | Ten Commandments |

 **Find the answers**

• What was the Exodus?

• Who did God promise that the Jews would be given a home of their own?

• Which set of laws are particularly important to Jews?

 **Learning about, learning from**

1. **a.** According to the Jewish scriptures, how long did it take God to create the world?
   **b.** What is the Sabbath Day?
   **c.** How do Jews follow the example of God on the Sabbath Day?

2. What happened during the Exodus?

3. Read the extract from the Ten Commandments in the box. What is the main difference between the God that Jews believe in and the gods of all the other nations?

4. **a.** What were the two sides of the agreement that God made with the Jews?
   **b.** The Jewish scriptures record that Jews have sometimes found it difficult to keep to their side of the agreement. Suggest why you think this is.

 **Extra activity**

Imagine you have been asked to give a talk on what Jews believe about God. What would you say?

# Allah

The **Shahadah** (the Muslim declaration of faith) begins by saying that there is only one God, Allah. This belief is at the heart of Islam. Allah does not share his power with anyone – He is unique, all-powerful and without equal.

## Allah

There is a great deal of information about Allah in the Qur'an. He is the creator of the universe who lifted up the heavens, put the mountains in place and created everything, both great and small. Allah provides water for the crops to grow and cultivates vines, olives, palms, orchards and all kinds of fruit for the pleasure of the people. He even looks after the flocks on the hillside. As the Qur'an says:

**A** The Shahadah recognises that there is one God, Allah

It is God who has made the night for you, that you may rest therein, and the day to see. Verily God is full of Grace and Bounty to all men. Yet most men give no thanks. Such is God, your Lord, the Creator of all things. There is no God but He; why do you then turn away from Him?

Muslims believe most people are ungrateful for all that Allah has provided. In a sense, though, this only makes the goodness of Allah even greater. His godly power enables Him to see all things – past, present and future. The Qur'an reminds its readers: 'A leaf does not fall without Allah knowing it.'

Because of Allah's greatness and goodness, Muslims are called to believe the message found in the Qur'an and to worship Allah.

## The names of Allah

Muslims express their feelings and beliefs about Allah by using certain names when they speak about Him. These names are recorded in the Qur'an. Allah has 99 such names in all, including:

* the Almighty
* the Compassionate
* the Forgiving
* the Wise
* the Creator
* the King
* the Giver.

Muslims believe it is impossible to worship Allah properly without remembering those in need. Those who fail to do this will be punished by Allah on the Day of Judgement. On this day, in particular, people singled out for condemnation are those who do not look after the orphan, those who not feed the hungry and the poor, those who steal the inheritance of others, and those who love wealth and neglect the needy.

**B** Because of the greatness of Allah, all Muslims kneel when they come into His presence

## In the glossary

Shahadah

### Find the answers

- What is the Shahadah and what does it say about Allah?

- How many different names of Allah are found in the Qur'an?

- Why will many people be punished by Allah on the Day of Judgement?

## From the Qur'an

The most important prayer in the Qur'an is found in its opening chapter:

*Praise be to Allah, Lord of the Universe,*
*The Compassionate, the Merciful,*
*Soverign of the Day of Judgement!*
*You alone we worship, and to You alone we turn for help.*
*Guide us to the straight path,*
*The path of those whom You have favoured,*
*Not of those who have incurred Your wrath,*
*Nor of those who have gone astray.*

### Learning about, learning from

1 Write down five things that Muslims believe about Allah.

2 Write a sentence to explain what each of the following titles given to Allah means. Use a dictionary if you need to.
   a. Compassionate.
   b. Supreme.
   c. Omnipotent.
   d. Omnipresent.
   e. Beneficent.

3 Find out more of the 99 names of Allah and make a wall display of them. Remember you cannot use any drawings of people or animals in your display, only words.

### Extra activity

Carry out some research to discover what zakah is. Explain how this is linked to what Muslims believe about Allah.

# Brahman

Hindus believe that everyone should be free to understand God in their own way and to pray to Him in any form they find helpful. Hindus, unlike followers of many other religions, make **murtis** (images) of God or paint pictures of Him to help them worship. As the pictures here show, Hindus have found many ways of representing God.

**A** There are many gods in Hinduism, but each of them points a way to the one God, Brahman

## Brahman

Brahman is the Hindu god who is over all other gods. Brahman is neither human nor animal, male nor female – Brahman is pure spirit from which everything comes and to which everything will finally return. The thousands of other gods and goddesses in Hinduism all show a different side of Brahman. Without them the Supreme Spirit, Brahman, would remain unknowable.

## The trimurti

Although there are many gods and goddesses in Hinduism, only three are involved in the creation, preservation and destruction of life. They are known as the **trimurti** (three gods):

- **Brahma**. Brahma is the Creator God with three heads. He needed each of his heads to search for his daughter, who had hidden from him when he wanted to seduce her. For this he was punished by the other gods. Brahma has few followers today.
- **Vishnu**. Vishnu is the Preserver God, who has already visited earth nine times in the form of Krishna and other gods. The visit of a god to earth is called an avatar. Krishna is the most popular of all the Hindu gods. His exploits on earth show him to have had a great sense of fun.
- **Shiva**. Shiva is the destroyer of evil, with three eyes and four arms. The eyes show his ability to look into the past, the present and the future. Two of his hands help him to keep the balance between creating and destroying life. His other two hands are outstretched to offer people protection and salvation. The drum in his left hand symbolises the creation of the universe. His feet are on the demon of ignorance, which must be destroyed if the people are to be saved.

## Ganesha

**Ganesha** is an important Hindu god. He brings good fortune and happiness to everyone who worships him. He is always shown with an elephant's head, which is a sign of great strength. In one of his four hands Ganesha holds a goad (a pointed stick) to show that he alone decides the fate of everyone. Ganesha is usually worshipped before any Hindu ceremony takes place.

**B** The many statues of the gods in Hinduism are intended to help the worshipper know the one God

## From the Upanishads

Although it is not possible to describe Brahman, the Upanishads, one of the Hindu holy books, speaks about Him as:
*Infinite in the east... in the south... in the west... in the north, above and below, and everywhere infinite... unlimited, unborn... not to be conceived.*

### In the glossary

| | |
|---|---|
| Brahma | Shiva |
| Ganesha | Trimurti |
| Murtis | Vishnu |

 **Find the answers**

- What is a murti?
- What is Brahman?
- Which three gods in Hinduism make up the trimurti?

 **Learning about, learning from**

1 Copy the picture of Ganesha (A) into your exercise book or file and label it using the information on these pages.

2 **a.** What is the trimurti?
   **b.** Write down two pieces of information about each of the members of the trimurti.

3 Choose one of the Hindu gods mentioned on these pages and write a paragraph about them.

 **Extra activity**

Read the quotation from the Upanishads in the box. In this extract, the writer describes what Brahman is *not* rather than what He *is*. Why do you think religious people sometimes find it easier to say what they do not believe about God rather than what they do?

# Nam and Waheguru

When Sikhism was founded by **Guru Nanak**, he wanted his message to be understood by everyone, educated and uneducated. He taught the people to believe in the Oneness of God, the Creator. If they accepted this belief, it would keep them from all evil and temptation. The name given to God, Nam, is a **mantra**. Through repeating this name, God takes root in the worshipper. His or her thoughts, words and deeds become an expression of God.

## The Mool Mantar

Guru Nanak knew that most of his listeners believed in many gods, which led them into many superstitions and fears. The **Guru** taught them the **Mool Mantar**, the statement of belief which comes at the beginning of the **Guru Granth Sahib** (see the box on the next page). Guru Angad, who succeeded Guru Nanak, taught Sikhs that everyone should learn the Mool Mantar by heart.

From the Mool Mantar Sikhs learn the basic message of Sikhism – that God is one and is everywhere. This message can be seen in the teachings of all the Gurus, the saints and the holy men. From them, Sikhs can also learn that God is in every area of life. It is only those who are spiritually blind who cannot see this.

## The all-powerful God

Sikhs believe that God created everything. He is still active in the world today, although he is also above and beyond it. As such, it is unthinkable that God should ever take on human form. He is all-powerful. He sees into the future and directs the affairs of those who have faith in him. Nothing can happen to those who trust God without God allowing it. God is the Divine Father who takes good care of His children. He listens to their prayers and gives them every possible blessing. He knows their deepest fears and understands and loves them.

Because God is so powerful, it is important that each Sikh should always keep the divine name in mind. A Sikh does this by repeating the word 'Waheguru' ('Wonderful Lord') over and over again during prayers and services. In this way, followers learn to think of their duty to love and serve God and others, so losing their naturally self-centred attitude towards life.

A The Sikh holy book, the Guru Granth Sahib, is a visible reminder of God, the true Guru

2 God and the gods

Nam and Waheguru

When Sikhism was founded by **Guru Nanak**, he wanted his message to be understood by everyone, educated and uneducated. He taught the people to believe in the Oneness of God, the Creator. If they accepted this belief, it would keep them from all evil and temptation. The name given to God, Nam, is a **mantra**. Through repeating this name, God takes root in the worshipper. His or her thoughts, words and deeds become an expression of God.

A The Sikh holy book, the Guru Granth Sahib, is a visible reminder of God, the true Guru

## The Mool Mantar

Guru Nanak knew that most of his listeners believed in many gods, which led them into many superstitions and fears. The **Guru** taught them the **Mool Mantar**, the statement of belief which comes at the beginning of the **Guru Granth Sahib** (see the box on the next page). Guru Angad, who succeeded Guru Nanak, taught Sikhs that everyone should learn the Mool Mantar by heart.

From the Mool Mantar Sikhs learn the basic message of Sikhism – that God is one and is everywhere. This message can be seen in the teachings of all the Gurus, the saints and the holy men. From them, Sikhs can also learn that God is in every area of life. It is only those who are spiritually blind who cannot see this.

## The all-powerful God

Sikhs believe that God created everything. He is still active in the world today, although he is also above and beyond it. As such, it is unthinkable that God should ever take on human form. He is all-powerful. He sees into the future and directs the affairs of those who have faith in him. Nothing can happen to those who trust God without God allowing it. God is the Divine Father who takes good care of His children. He listens to their prayers and gives them every possible blessing. He knows their deepest fears and understands and loves them.

Because God is so powerful, it is important that each Sikh should always keep the divine name in mind. A Sikh does this by repeating the word 'Waheguru' ('Wonderful Lord') over and over again during prayers and services. In this way, followers learn to think of their duty to love and serve God and others, so losing their naturally self-centred attitude towards life.

26

**B** Sikhs take off their shoes when they enter God's presence in the gurdwara

## The Mool Mantar

*There is One God Whose Name is Truth,*
*God is the Creator, and without fear and without hate.*
*God is timeless.*
*God's Spirit is throughout the universe.*
*God is not born, nor will die to be born again.*
*God is self-existent.*
*By the grace of the Gurus God is made known to mankind.*

**In the glossary**

| | |
|---|---|
| Guru | Guru Nanak |
| Guru Granth Sahib | Mantra |
| | Mool Mantar |

 **Find the answers**

- What is the basic Sikh belief?
- What is the name for the Sikh statement of belief?
- How does a Sikh try to keep the name of God constantly in mind?

 **Learning about, learning from**

1 **a.** What does Waheguru mean?
  **b.** What do Sikhs hope to achieve by repeating it constantly?

2 **a.** Which two names do Sikhs use for God?
  **b.** What do Sikhs believe about God?

3 How does a Sikh find that believing in God helps him or her in their everyday life?

 **Extra activity**

Read the quotation from the Mool Mantar in the box.
**a.** The Mool Mantar promises many things for the person who makes the praise of God their normal activity. What are they?
**b.** How do you think praising God might take away the fear of dying?

# Around birth

## Introduction

People the world over are excited by the birth of a new baby. In many countries people send cards and hold parties to mark the occasion. The mother and father have followed the progress of the baby through nine months of pregnancy, but there is always unease until the baby is born. In many parts of the world it is still risky to give birth. Both parents and relations breathe a huge sigh of relief when the baby is born safely.

### The gift of new life

For parents who hold strong religious beliefs, the birth of a baby has special significance. The major religions all teach their followers that a new baby is a gift from God, a new creation. The word 'gift' is particularly important. The parents have been given their new baby by God as a gift. Along with the gift comes the responsibility of bringing up the baby in the teachings and traditions of the parents' religious faith.

This responsibility starts early. Each religion has some ceremony when the child is taken to the place of worship and presented to God. This gives everyone, parents and members of the congregation alike, the opportunity to thank God for the gift of new life. In the Baptist Church, for example, a service is held during which the child's life is 'dedicated' to God. In many other Christian Churches the baby is baptised, during which water is sprinkled or poured over it. From this time the child becomes a member of the Christian Church.

In many religions children are the only source of 'wealth' that really matters. For example, the Jewish scriptures speak for parents of all religions when they refer to sons as being a heritage from God (see the box on the next page). Modern parents, though, would stress that daughters are valued as highly as well.

# In this unit

## In this unit you will read about the following:

- The celebration of **infant baptism** in most Christian Churches and the promises that are made for a child born into a Christian family.

- The importance of **circumcision** for members of the Jewish community.

- The important ceremonies carried out in a Muslim family during the first few days of a baby's life.

- The early **samskaras** carried out before and after birth in a Hindu family, including the naming of the child, an event which has considerable importance.

- The Sikh naming ceremony.

## From the Jewish scriptures

These words from the Jewish scriptures emphasise the importance of children within the family:

*Sons are a heritage from the Lord, children a reward from him. Like arrows in the hands of a warrior are sons born in one's youth. Blessed is the man whose quiver is full of them.*

### In the glossary

Circumcision          Samskaras
Infant baptism

# Infant baptism

When members of the early Christian Church began to make new converts in the Roman Empire, they baptised them. Baptism showed that their sins had been washed away. This was a sign of their new faith in Christ. There is no evidence, however, to suggest that they ever baptised babies. Centuries later infant baptism, or christening, became the usual practice in Roman Catholic, Orthodox and Anglican Churches. There are some Churches, such as the Baptists, which baptise only adults. Their service is called believer's baptism and we will look at this on pages 44 and 45.

## The service

The service of infant baptism takes place in church around the **font**. This is like a bowl on a stand and it holds the water for baptism. Its position near the church entrance symbolises the belief that baptism is the door through which babies pass to become members of the Church.

During the service the baby is sprinkled with water three times as a symbol of forgiveness in the name of God the Father, God the Son and God the Holy Spirit. In the Orthodox Church the clothes of the baby are removed and it is submerged beneath the water during baptism.

As the baby is too young to speak for itself, two godparents and the parents speak on its behalf. During the service they are asked three questions by the priest and, in reply, they make promises on behalf of the child:

> *Priest:* Do you turn to Christ?
> *Answer:* I turn to Christ.
> *Priest:* Do you repent of your sins?
> *Answer:* I repent of my sins.
> *Priest:* Do you renounce evil?
> *Answer:* I renounce evil.

Some years later the child will have the opportunity of renewing these vows for themselves. This happens during the

**A** When a baby is baptised it becomes a member of God's family, the Church

**B** Baptists do not believe in infant baptism – they dedicate their babies to God in a simple service instead

service of confirmation (see pages 42 and 43). In the Orthodox Church, however, baptism and confirmation take place in the same service, called **chrismation**.

Then, as the priest makes the 'sign of the cross' on the baby's forehead with water, he or she says:

> I baptise you in the Name of the Father, and of the Son and of the Holy Spirit.

The priest may then give the child's parents a lighted candle, saying to them:

> This is to show that you have passed from darkness to light.

to which the congregation replies:

> Shine as a light in the world to the glory of God the Father.

Each member of the congregation takes on the responsibility of helping to bring up the child in the Christian faith by surrounding him or her with their love.

---

### In the glossary

Chrismation          Font

---

## What is baptism?

A Church of England prayer book says this about infant baptism:

*Children who are too young to profess the Christian faith are baptised on the understanding that they are brought up as Christians within the family of the Church.*

### Find the answers

- What are the two forms of baptism which are used within the Christian Church?

- What is the font and why is it often placed near the door of a church?

- What is the link between the services of infant baptism and confirmation?

### Learning about, learning from

**1 a.** What is infant baptism?
   **b.** Name two Churches that carry out infant baptism.

**2 a.** Do you think it is right for parents to have their baby baptised before it is old enough to understand what is being done? Explain your answer.
   **b.** If you were a Christian parent, would you have your children baptised? Explain your answer.

### Extra activity

Recently a vicar refused to baptise a baby because his parents did not go to church. Do you think the vicar was right? Explain your answer.

# Circumcision

The arrival of a new baby into a Jewish family is greeted with great joy. If the baby is a girl, the father is called up to read from the **Torah** in the synagogue. He also announces the name of the baby to the congregation. If the child is a boy, the baby must be circumcised. Circumcision means the removal of the foreskin, the skin covering the tip of the penis.

## Abraham and circumcision

Circumcision is an ancient custom that is still carried out by Jews today. In the opening book of the Jewish scriptures it says that Abraham made an agreement with God. Under this agreement Jews promised to keep God's laws and God promised to protect the Jewish nation. As a sign of the bond between them, God told Abraham to circumcise all the males in his large family – 318 of them in all. Anyone who was not prepared to be circumcised could not belong to the Jewish family (see the box on the next page).

## Circumcision today

Every Jewish boy must be circumcised on the eighth day of his life. Traditionally it was the father's responsibility to carry out this duty, following in the footsteps of Abraham. In recent times, however, it is almost always a professional circumciser, called a mohel, who does it. As with many other Jewish religious ceremonies this one, called the brit milah, is carried out in the home rather than in the synagogue.

The baby is carried into the room by a female relative or friend of the family. The child's mother does not attend her son's circumcision. It is the grandfather who holds the baby while the circumcision is carried out. The mohel removes the foreskin of the boy's penis with a sharp knife. The father then recalls the words spoken by God to Abraham when he says to everyone:

> God has commanded me to introduce my son into the covenant of our father, Abraham.

Everyone present responds with the prayer:

> As he entered into the covenant, so may he enter into a study of the Torah, marriage and a life of good deeds.

The boy is then given a special Jewish name, which he will use on religious occasions. The name is followed by 'ben' ('son of') and then the name of his father. The circumcision is followed by a party attended by all members of the family.

**A** This sculpture is a reminder of the Jewish belief that God protects every young life

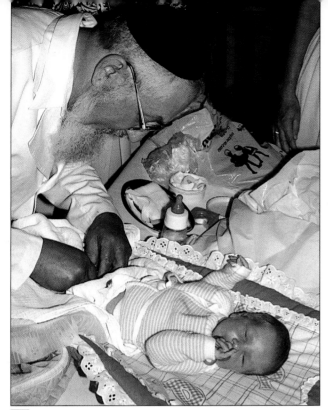

**B** Circumcision is the oldest Jewish religious practice still carried out today

# Every male to be circumcised

These are God's words to Abraham about circumcision:
*This is my covenant with you and with your descendants after you, the covenant you are to keep. Every male among you shall be circumcised. You are to undergo circumcision, and it will be a sign of the covenant between me and you. For the generations to come every male among you who is eight days old must be circumcised... Any uncircumcised male, who has not been circumcised in the flesh, will be cut off from his people; he has broken my covenant.*

---

**In the glossary**

Torah

---

 **Find the answers**

- What is circumcision?

- When is circumcision carried out in a Jewish family and where is the ceremony usually held?

- What does the Jewish word 'ben' mean?

 **Learning about, learning from**

**1** In these sentences the heads and tails have been mixed up. Unscramble them and write down the correct versions in your exercise book or file.

| | |
|---|---|
| Jews have their male children circumcised | a professional Jewish circumciser. |
| The ceremony of circumcision | circumcision of all Abraham's male children and older members of his household. |
| As a sign of the bond between God and Jews, He commanded | |
| | on the eighth day after birth. |
| A mohel is | is called brit milah. |

**2 a.** Which other ways could be used to show that people are members of a religious faith?
**b.** Why have Jews continued to use circumcision as a sign of their faith?

**Extra activity**

An old Jewish saying says that three people are involved in the birth of a baby – the mother, the father and God. What do you think this saying is teaching?

# Aqiqah

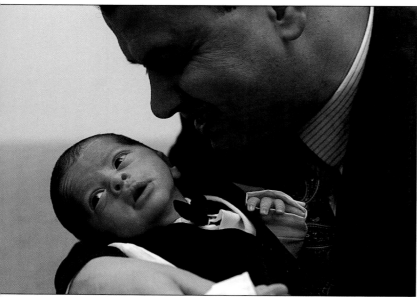

**A** It is important that the first word a Muslim baby hears should be God's name, Allah

A Muslim baby is bathed as soon as it is born. Then the father welcomes it into the family by whispering the Shahadah into his or her ear. This is followed by the **adhan** (see the box on the next page). The first words that a baby hears are very important because they mark the beginning of religious education. The child will hear the adhan many times during its lifetime – it is the Muslim call to prayer.

## Birth ceremonies

Soon after birth an older member of the child's family performs the tahnik ceremony. A small soft piece of a date is put into the baby's mouth to symbolise the hope that it will develop a sweet nature, and a **du'a** (prayer) is said on the baby's behalf. Then, seven days after birth, the important ceremony of **aqiqah** takes place. Passages from the Qur'an are read before the father announces the child's name. Many boys are named after one of Allah's 99 names or the prophet **Muhammad**. Names like Abdul (servant)

and Mahmood are popular among Muslim believers. Girls' names might be chosen from Muhammad's wives or daughters. Muslim parents often seek the advice of grandparents before making their final choice.

Two important acts take place as part of the aqiqah:

- The baby's head is shaved and gold or silver equivalent to the weight of the hair is given away to charity. The shaving of the baby's head is a symbolic act to take away the uncleanness of birth as well as to encourage the hair to grow back more thickly. The hair is treated with great respect because it is part of a human being. It is buried carefully after it has been weighed.
- In the case of a baby boy, two goats or a sheep are sacrificed, and for a baby girl one animal is killed. The animal that is sacrificed must be perfect. One third of the meat is given away to the poor and the remainder is eaten by relatives.

## Khitan

Khitan is the circumcision (removal of the foreskin of the penis) of a Muslim boy. Muslim boys are often circumcised on the eighth day after birth. This custom, however, can wait until the child is much older. Muslims believe that God instructed the prophet Ibrahim (Abraham) to circumcise all the males in his household. The Prophet Muhammad told his followers that all Muslim male children should be circumcised by the time they reach their tenth birthday.

# The adhan

This is the Muslim call to prayer: *God is the greatest. God is the greatest. God is the greatest. God is the greatest. I bear witness that there is no God but Allah. I bear witness that there is no God but Allah. I bear witness that Muhammad is the messenger of Allah. I bear witness that Muhammad is the messenger of Allah. Come to prayer. Come to prayer. Come to security. Come to security. God is the most great. God is the most great. There is no God but Allah.*

**B** A Muslim baby's head is shaved to symbolise the removal of all uncleanness from the child

## In the glossary

| | |
|---|---|
| Adhan | Du'a |
| Aqiqah | Muhammad |

## Find the answers

- When does the aqiqah ceremony take place?

- How many names does Allah have which are known to human beings?

- How is the name of a Muslim child chosen?

## Learning about, learning from

1  **a.** What happens to a Muslim child soon after birth?
   **b.** Why is it important that this happens as soon as possible?
   **c.** On which other occasions will a Muslim hear the same words?

2  **a.** Why do you think Muslims believe it is important that a newborn baby should hear the adhan?
   **b.** What does this tell you about the way Muslim children are brought up?

3  **a.** What is aqiqah?
   **b.** Which two important acts take place as a part of aqiqah?

## Extra activity

The animal that is killed to give thanks for birth has to be perfect. Why is this important?

# Hindu birth ceremonies

**A** Three samskaras take place before the baby is born

## Samskaras

Hindus believe that everybody passes through 16 important stages on their journey from birth to death. Each stage is marked with a special religious ceremony called a samskara.

The first samskara takes place even before a baby is conceived and two more are carried out before it is born. The first is to make sure that the woman can have a baby and the following two are to make sure that the baby is growing properly in the womb.

## Birth

The birth of a baby is always greeted by Hindus with great excitement. The priest is informed of the exact time of birth so that a horoscope can be drawn up for the child. Hindus believe that the stars are an important influence at certain times in a baby's life.

The fourth samskara is performed shortly after the baby is born. The baby is washed and the sacred syllable, **aum**, is traced on its tongue using a golden pen dipped in honey. This represents the most important Hindu gods – Brahma, Vishnu and Shiva.

## Naming

Hindu parents do not register the birth of their baby until after the fifth samskara, which takes place on the tenth day after the baby is born. Using the birth horoscope, the priest is able to suggest certain syllables to form the baby's name. His or her name will play an important part in the child's life. Prayers are recited asking that the child will be given both strength and wisdom for the life ahead. As with other Hindu ceremonies, this one takes place in front of a sacred fire to symbolise the purity and presence of God. The baby is washed and dressed in new clothes.

## Feeling the sunlight

Soon afterwards, the baby is taken outside to see the sun for the first time. For most Hindu mothers, the first outing with the baby is to the local temple where she can give thanks for the safe birth. Offerings of flowers, fruit and incense are placed in front of the different statues in the temple. In some families special prayers are also said when the child reaches six months of age, to mark the time when solid foods are eaten for the first time.

## Karma

At around the time of a boy's first birthday his hair is cut off. This symbolises the removal of bad **karma**. This means that the consequences of bad actions from a past life are taken away and the child now has a clean slate with which to begin the present life. The hair is collected together carefully because it is part of human life.

Sometimes it is burned in the sacred fire, but other Hindus prefer to bury it close to their home village or to scatter it in the waters of the River Ganges.

**B** The sacred syllable is traced on the baby's tongue soon after it is born

---

**In the glossary**

Aum          Karma

---

 **Find the answers**

- What is a samskara?

- How many samskaras are there in the life of a Hindu?

- What happens at the fifth samskara?

---

**Learning about, learning from**

1 When a Hindu speaks the sacred syllable, he or she finds themselves drawn into union with God.
   **a.** What is the sacred syllable?
   **b.** Why is the sacred syllable written on the tongue of every newborn Hindu baby?
   **c.** Suggest a reason why it is written in honey.

2 What are the main hopes and fears expressed through the various Hindu birth ceremonies?

3 **a.** What do you think have been and will be the most important stages in your life?
   **b.** Explain what you understand to be the importance of each stage.
   **c.** Compare your ideas with those of other people in your class. Explain why events take on a greater or lesser importance for different people.

---

 **Extra activity**

The birth and naming of a Hindu child are accompanied by many ceremonies. What value do they have for Hindus?

# The Sikh naming ceremony

When Sikh parents are ready, they bring their new baby to the **gurdwara** to be presented before the Guru Granth Sahib. They do this to thank God for the child's safe delivery and so that the child might receive his or her name.

## Amrit

The **granthi** prepares the **amrit** for the ceremony by mixing sugar and water. As he does so, he reads out five verses from the scriptures. At the same time, he stirs the mixture with a short sword. Then the special prayer used in most Sikh services, the **Ardas**, is recited. The person leading the service ends it with the words that you will find in the box on the next page.

After reciting the prayer, amrit is dropped on to the baby's lips. The mother is given the remainder to drink. The name of the child is decided by opening the holy book. Its first name will begin with the first letter on the page on which the holy book falls open. If the child is a boy, 'Singh' (lion) is added to the name; if a girl, 'Kaur' (princess).

In thanks to God for the gift of the child, the parents present a romalla to the gurdwara. This is a cloth that is used to cover the Guru Granth Sahib when it is not being read in the gurdwara.

## Responsibilities

After the naming ceremony, **karah parshad** is distributed to everyone in the gurdwara. A little of this holy food is placed on the baby's lips to show that he or she is now a member of the Sikh community. From now on, the parents take on the solemn responsibility to make sure they raise their child in the Sikh faith. The baby is given a kara (steel bracelet), which symbolises the unity of the community that it has joined and is also a reminder of the oneness of God. This will be worn on the right wrist for the rest of the child's life. The naming ceremony ends, as with all Sikh services, with a meal for the whole congregation in the **langar**. The ingredients for this meal are provided by the child's parents as a thanks offering to God.

The parents of Sikh children have two other responsibilities as a child grows up:

- If the child is a boy, he has to wear the traditional **turban** from his boyhood onwards. He starts to wear it as soon as he is old enough to tie it for himself. It is the parents' responsibility to make sure this happens.
- The parents must make sure their children do not have their hair cut. Long hair is a sign of devotion to God in Sikhism.

**A** The gurdwara plays an important role in the lives of Sikhs

**B** The Guru Granth Sahib plays an important part in choosing the name of a Sikh child

## A Sikh prayer

This prayer is said during the naming ceremony:
*I present this child and with thy Grace*
*I administer him amrit.*
*May he be a true Sikh,*
*May he devote himself to the service of his fellow men and motherland.*
*May he be inspired with devotion,*
*May the holy food be acceptable to the congregation.*
*By the ever-increasing glory of your name may the whole creation be blessed.*

### In the glossary

| | |
|---|---|
| Amrit | Karah parshad |
| Ardas | Langar |
| Granthi | Turban |
| Gurdwara | |

 **Find the answers**

- What is amrit?
- What is a romalla?
- What is karah parshad?

**Learning about, learning from**

1 Explain how the name of a Sikh child is chosen.

2 Why should a Sikh boy be able to tie his own turban before he is allowed to wear one?

3 Guru Nanak was the founder of Sikhism. He taught his followers that family ties, no matter how important they are, could not help a person on the path to salvation. Every person must make their own peace with God. He said: 'The wife, the son, brothers, no one shall hold my hand. At last when I shall fall and the time of my last prayer shall come, there shall be none to rescue me.'
   a. What do you think Guru Nanak meant when he said 'when I shall fall'?
   b. Why does he not want to depend on his family for salvation at that time?

 **Extra activity**

Using the Sikh prayer in the box, describe what things people pray for the child at his or her naming ceremony.

# Growing up

## 4 Introduction

The process of growing up is a long and sometimes difficult one. As each child passes through infancy and then puberty, their parents carry a heavy responsibility for their upbringing. For those who come from religious families, there are special ceremonies linked to this important time.

### Responsibilities

One of the most important responsibilities carried by religious parents is to introduce their children to the beliefs and way of life their religion offers. Children cannot be made to believe, but religious parents always hope their children will grow up to share their own faith.

If this does happen, though, it will not be by accident. From birth onwards the home is the main place where religious education takes place. In many religions it is the mother, in particular, who carries out this task. In the case of boys, however, once the child grows older this responsibility often shifts to the father. In Judaism, for example, it is the father who guides his son towards his **bar mitzvah**.

### Teaching the children

To supplement the teaching that goes on at home, most religions run their own schools that give religious education to children. Most Christian churches have their Sunday schools where the children are taught each week about the Christian faith and the Bible. Each synagogue runs its own school for Jewish children to teach them about their religion. They also learn Hebrew there because this is the language in which the Jewish scriptures were written. Hindu children usually learn about the duties and responsibilities of their faith from a guru.

All this instruction and teaching is designed to lead the child towards an important event – the ceremony that recognises publicly that they are now an adult and no longer a child. The age at which this takes place varies from religion to religion. In some, the age is fixed rigidly, but in others it is more flexible. In Judaism a boy's bar mitzvah usually takes place on the first Sabbath Day after his thirteenth birthday. The **sacred thread** ceremony for Hindu boys can take place at any time between the seventh and thirteenth birthdays.

These ceremonies mean that an important line has been crossed. They mark the fact that the person has now become a full member of their religious community in their own right. Of course, they still have much to learn, but they are now responsible for making their own spiritual decisions.

# In this unit

## In this unit you will read about the following:

- The Christian ceremony of confirmation. This is the opportunity for people to 'confirm' the promises that others made for them when they were baptised.

- The Christian service of believer's baptism. This ceremony is conducted by the Baptist Church and a few others. Baptism is reserved for adulthood when a person is able to decide to follow Christ for themselves.

- The Jewish ceremonies of bar mitvah and **bat mitzvah**. In bar mitzvah Jewish boys and in bat mizvah some Jewish girls are publicly recognised as adults.

- Although there is no specific Muslim ceremony to acknowledge that children is now an adult, bringing up children is a matter of great importance in the Muslim faith.

- Receiving the sacred thread is an important ceremony in Hinduism. The thread, which the boy wears for the rest of his life, is a visible symbol that he is 'twice-born'. Only boys from the highest group in India have traditionally received the sacred thread, but in Britain today many Hindus perform this ceremony.

- The **Amrit Sanskar** ceremony in Sikhism, which marks the time when a Sikh becomes a member of the **Khalsa**, the brotherhood of committed believers.

## Growing up

In the Bible, the writer of the book of Proverbs says:
*Teach a child how he should live and he will remember it all his life.*

### In the glossary

| | |
|---|---|
| Amrit Sanskar | Khalsa |
| Bar mitzvah | Sacred thread |
| Bat mitzvah | |

# Confirmation

Confirmation is celebrated in the Anglican, Roman Catholic and Orthodox Churches. To Roman Catholic and Orthodox believers, it is one of the seven sacraments, or 'mysteries' as Orthodox Christians prefer to call them. In the Orthodox Church, infant baptism and confirmation are carried out in the same service, called chrismation. Some people, though, are much older when they are confirmed.

## The service

The importance of the confirmation service is shown by the fact that it is almost always carried out by a bishop. During the service he asks each person being confirmed three questions. The questions mirror those the parents and godparents were asked when the person was baptised as a baby:

*Bishop:* You have come here to be confirmed. You stand in the presence of God and His Church. With your own mouth and from your own heart you must declare your allegiance to Christ and your rejection of all that is evil. Therefore, I ask you these questions: Do you turn to Christ?

*Answer:* I turn to Christ.
*Bishop:* Do you repent of your sins?
*Answer:* I repent of my sins.
*Bishop:* Do you renounce evil?
*Answer:* I renounce evil.

The bishop then asks three more questions:

*Bishop:* Do you believe and trust in God the Father who made the world?
*Answer:* I believe and trust in him.
*Bishop:* Do you believe and trust in Jesus Christ, his Son, who redeemed mankind?
*Answer:* I believe and trust in him.
*Bishop:* Do you believe and trust in the Holy Spirit who gives life to the people of God?
*Answer:* I believe and trust in him.

After this, each person kneels in front of the bishop, who lays his hands on their forehead. He prays for them: 'Confirm, O Lord, your servant with your Holy Spirit.' The 'laying on of hands' is an old Christian tradition to show that a person has received the Holy Spirit. The Holy Spirit will now help them in their Christian life.

The service is often followed by the sacrament of Holy Communion. This is the time when newly confirmed Christians kneel at the altar to take their first communion. Relatives and friends give them gifts, such as a prayer book or a special Bible. From this time onwards the person tries to live the Christian life and to take Holy Communion regularly, especially at the important festivals of **Christmas** and **Easter**.

**A** The confirmation service is almost always carried out by a bishop

### In the glossary
Christmas       Easter

**B** The 'laying on of hands' is at the centre of the confirmation service

# From the confirmation service

During the confirmation service the bishop tells each person:
*Beloved in Christ, at your baptism you were received into God's family, the Church. You have grown in the knowledge and love of your Lord. You have heard Christ saying to you, as he said to his first disciples, 'Follow me'. You have already responded to his call, and you come now, by your own choice, publicly to renounce evil and profess your faith in him. You are now to be confirmed.*

 **Find the answers**

- In which Churches is confirmation carried out?

- Who carries out the confirmation service and what does this show?

- Why does the bishop lay his hands on the head of every person being confirmed?

 **Learning about, learning from**

1  **a.** What is confirmation?
   **b.** What is confirmation called in the Orthodox Church?
   **c.** What is the main difference between confirmation in the Orthodox Church and confirmation in the other Churches that also celebrate it?

2  **a.** How important a step do you think confirmation is to those taking part in it?
   **b.** At what times in your life do you think you may stand up in front of other people to tell them something important about yourself?

 **Extra activity**

People can be confirmed at any age. In the Roman Catholic Church you can be as young as seven years old; in the Anglican Church you are unlikely to be younger than twelve and usually older. What do you think is a suitable age for someone to take a decision about their own spiritual life? Explain your answer.

# Believer's baptism

While most Christian denominations baptise babies, the Baptist Church baptises only adults. Soon after a baby is born it is brought to church by his or her parents and dedicated to God. From the age of 12 onwards the person can ask to be baptised after they have made their own commitment to follow Jesus.

In most Baptist churches there is a pool in the floor at the front, which is filled with water for the baptism. Some churches, though, prefer to carry out their baptisms in the local stream, river or sea. Those who are baptised in the open air are following the example of Jesus, who was baptised by John the Baptist in the River Jordan. You can read about this in the box on the next page.

## The service

In church the minister stands in the water to receive the person wishing to be baptised. The person has already spoken to the church congregation to describe how they became a Christian. The minister tells them:

> Baptism unites us with Christ through faith, as we die with him to sin, and rise with him in newness of life. The washing of our bodies is the outward and visible sign that our souls are cleansed from sin through Jesus Christ our Lord.

The person either stands or kneels in the water, before being gently rocked backwards until their whole body is beneath the water. This is called baptism by immersion. Then, as the person comes up out of the pool, the congregation sing a hymn.

## Baptism as a symbol

Nothing magical or mysterious happens when a person is baptised. It is the meaning behind the event and not the event itself that is important. Water is a symbol of washing and new life. Each part of the service has symbolic significance:

- By entering the water the person shows that they are leaving their sinful life behind. Their sins have been forgiven because of their faith in Christ. Just as Jesus died on the cross, so they are 'dying' in their old life.
- In the moment or two they are under the water, the person is showing that their old life is ended. Just as Jesus spent three days buried in the tomb, so they are 'buried' with Christ.

**A** Baptists are following the example of Jesus when they choose to be baptised

- As they come up out of the water, the person shows that they are now entering into the new life that Jesus came to bring. Just as Jesus returned to life after three days, so the baptised person has entered into the resurrection life of Jesus. They are now 'spiritually alive'.

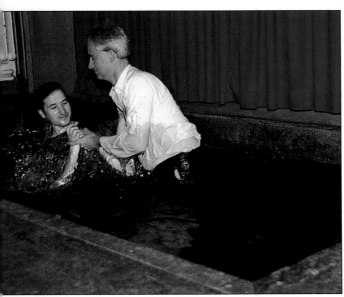

**B** The waters of baptism are a symbol of the washing away of a person's sins

## The baptism of Jesus

This is how one Gospel writer, Mark, described the baptism of Jesus:

*At that time Jesus came from Nazareth in Galilee and was baptised by John in the Jordan. As Jesus was coming up out of the water, he saw heaven being torn open and the Spirit descending on him like a dove. And a voice from heaven: 'You are my Son, whom I love; with you I am well pleased.'*

 **Find the answers**

- Whose example are Baptists following when they are baptised as adults?

- What does a person do before they go down into the pool to be baptised?

- What happens as a person leaves the pool after being baptised?

 **Learning about, learning from**

1  a. Make a series of three drawings to show the different stages of believer's baptism.
   b. Write two sentences underneath each drawing to explain what is happening.

2  Imagine you have just been present at the baptism of a friend. Describe what you saw. Include a sentence or two about the significance of the service for your friend.

3  In picture B the man is just coming out of the water after having been baptised. What is this person saying about their own life, and the future, as they leave the water?

 **Extra activity**

The early Christians always carried out baptism in running water, so this ceremony was usually performed in a stream or the sea. Suggest a reason why running water was thought to be necessary for baptism.

# Bar mitzvah and bat mitzvah

Each week, from the age of four, Jewish children spend time in their local synagogue learning about their faith and the Hebrew language. In all synagogues, a boy celebrates his bar mitzvah ('son of the commandment') on the first Sabbath Day after his thirteenth birthday. From this age he is considered old enough to take responsibility for his own future spiritual decisions. In some synagogues a girl also becomes a bat mitzvah ('daughter of the commandment'), although this takes place after her twelfth birthday.

## Bar mitzvah

The bar mitzvah is a great family occasion, with many relatives and friends invited. During the service in the synagogue the boy is called up to read

from the Torah scroll in public for the first time. A metal finger pointer, called a yad, is used to follow the passage so that there is no human contact with the holy text itself. To read from the scriptures in this way is a great spiritual privilege. Both the boy and his father then offer their own prayers to God. The father says a blessing:

> Blessed be He [God] who frees me from the responsibility of this boy.

The boy asks for God's help that he might follow in the footsteps of his ancestors and obey God's holy commandments. He says a prayer like this:

> Heavenly Father, at this sacred time in my life, I stand before thee in the midst of this holy congregation to declare my duty ever to return to Thee in daily prayer and to observe the commandments of Thy laws by which a man may live worthily. I pray humbly and hopefully before Thee to grant me Thy gracious help.

The boy is given two sacred objects to show that he is now accepted as an adult within the Jewish community:

- The **tefillin**. These are two small leather boxes which are tied with a strap around the left arm and the forehead – the nearest points to the heart and the brain. The tefillin contain important passages from the scriptures, including the **Shema**, which is written on parchment in Hebrew. Each worshipper wears them for morning prayers.
- The **tallit** (prayer shawl). This is made of silk or wool with fringes at the ends. Each fringe has 613 strands to remind the worshipper that there are 613 commandments in total in the Torah. Like the tefillin, the tallit is worn for morning prayers.

**A** In the Jewish community a boy's bar mitzvah marks his arrival into adulthood

## Bat mitzvah

In some synagogues a bat mitzvah is held for girls. As part of this ceremony, each girl is allowed to read a passage from the Torah in Hebrew. In most synagogues, however, girls have a **bat chayil** ('daughter of worth') ceremony instead. At this, girls do not read from the Torah – that is the responsibility of the males in the congregation. It is important, though, for girls to learn how to run a good Jewish home and this forms an important part of instruction for the bat chayil.

**B** It is important that Jewish children learn Hebrew, the language in which their scriptures are written

## The words of blessing

Here are the words of blessing that are used at every bar mitzvah:
*The Lord bless thee and keep thee. The Lord make His face to shine upon thee and be gracious unto thee; the Lord lift up the light of His countenance upon thee and give thee peace.*

### In the glossary

| | |
|---|---|
| Bat chayil | Tallit |
| Shema | Tefillin |

### Find the answers

- What is the bar mitzvah?
- What is the bat mitzvah?
- What is the bat chayil?

### Learning about, learning from

1 Why do you think a bar mitzvah is important:
   **a.** to the boy?
   **b.** to the boy's parents?
   **c.** to the Jewish community?

2 Why is it important for a young Jew to learn Hebrew?

3 What do you think are the advantages and disadvantages of being considered to be an adult at the age of twelve or thirteen?

### Extra activity

Imagine you are a Jewish boy or girl who is about to have your bar mitzvah or bat mitzvah. Write a paragraph describing a day that marks a very important milestone in your life.

# Growing up in a Muslim family

There is no special ceremony in Islam to mark the time when a Muslim child becomes an adult. Instead, the emphasis within the Muslim community is on the continual training and education of a child, which begins at birth. From that moment nothing is done in the child's presence that could damage his or her spiritual growth. To help this growth, it is important that the child should hear frequent quotations from the Qur'an. In this way it is hoped that the teaching of the holy book will become almost second nature to them before he or she becomes an adult.

## Education

As soon as a child is old enough, they learn how to pray and are taught passages from the Qur'an which are learned by heart. Reading and learning the scriptures and praying are at the very heart of Muslim spirituality. Each child must know, for example, what prayers to say before they eat, drink, wear new clothes or go to bed. By saying the right prayer at the right time, each child learns to follow the Muslim way of life.

The Prophet Muhammad told of the way that Muslim parents should bring up their children when he said:

> The best gift which a father gives to his children is that of a good education and good manners.

## Teaching good manners

In a Muslim family it is a religious duty to teach each child the manners that are expected of them. Parents do this by setting their children a good example each day and by living out the Muslim faith in front of them. The story of Hazrat Umar-Abu-Salma shows how children best learn from the example set by others. He was brought up as a child by the Prophet Muhammad. Later, he wrote about something that had happened in his early years:

> Once, during my childhood, I was sitting in the lap of the Holy Prophet eating something. I was eating from all sides of the plate. The Holy Prophet advised me to say 'Bismillah' [in the name of Allah] and then eat with my right hand and from just before me. Since then I have made it my habit.

**A** It is important that boys should read and study the Qur'an from an early age

## Telling stories

Young children love stories and storytelling is an important part of Muslim childhood. The stories that the children are told, however, must be chosen with great care. Parents must avoid telling their children stories about demons, fairies, witches and any kind of imaginary creations. Muslims believe these stories plant false and damaging ideas into the minds of children. Parents must also avoid putting false ideas about Allah or the world in which they live into the minds of young children. Children must not be made afraid of things that do not exist.

 Reading the scriptures is at the heart of Islam

 **Learning about, learning from**

1  **a.** How are Muslim parents expected to protect their children as they grow up?
   **b.** What duties do Muslim parents have towards their children?
   **c.** How do Muslim parents carry out these duties?

2  Muhammad taught that from the age of ten all children are old enough to take responsibility for their own religious worship. He said: 'Children are to be taught how to offer prayer when they become seven years old and encouraged when they reach the age of ten (if they show slackness in offering prayer).' Were you old enough to make decisions about your own religious beliefs at the age of ten? Explain your answer.

3  Storytelling is an important part of a young child's life in Islam. What should parents avoid when telling their children stories? Explain your answer.

### Find the answers

- When do Muslims start to train their children in the Muslim way of life?

- What must a young Muslim child hear frequently as he or she grows up?

- What, according to the Prophet Muhammad, is the best gift that a father can give to his children?

### Extra activity

Muhammad taught all parents: 'When your children should start speaking make them learn that there is no God but Allah and Muhammad is the messenger of Allah.' This is the basic statement of faith (the Shahadah) for all Muslim believers. Why did Muhammad say it should be taught as soon as children learn to talk?

# The sacred thread ceremony

The most important ceremony in Hinduism is that of the sacred thread. This is the tenth samskara in a Hindu's life and can take place at any time between a boy's seventh and thirteenth birthdays.

## The three debts

A boy is not a Hindu in his own right until a priest has laid the sacred thread across his shoulder. It shows that he is old enough to receive his spiritual education from a guru. The three strands of the thread remind him that he has three debts to pay:

- a debt to God
- a debt to his parents and ancestors
- a debt to the wise men (gurus) of his religion, whose teachings will guide him through life.

**A** A Hindu child grows up knowing that he or she owes a great debt to their parents

The strands are tied together with a special knot called the Brahma granthi or spiritual knot. Apart from changing the thread from time to time, the boy will wear it for the rest of his life. It passes across the left shoulder and down to the right hip. The only time it is removed is when he is in mourning for a dead relative. It is a constant reminder that he is spiritually 'twice-born'. The first birth was when he entered the world from his mother's womb, and the second was when he began to learn the way of salvation from his guru.

## The ceremony

The ceremony can take place in either the home or the temple. However, it is more likely to be in the temple because the holy fire can be lit more easily there. The boy washes his body to show that he is starting a new stage in his life and has his head shaved. He wears new or clean clothes for the ceremony to symbolise the new life that he is beginning.

The holy fire around which the ceremony takes place is a symbol of the presence of God. It is lit for all Hindu ceremonies. During this ceremony the child's father hands him over to the guru for his future spiritual training. The boy promises that he will be a good pupil, obey his teacher and be self-disciplined. He then places a garland over the head of his teacher as a sign of respect. In the past the child left home to study with his guru, but this rarely happens now. Instead, the boy accepts that he must:

- pray three times each day
- perform the necessary religious ceremonies
- study the sacred Hindu scriptures.

He will do this until he is ready to pass on to the next stage in his spiritual development – that of being a householder.

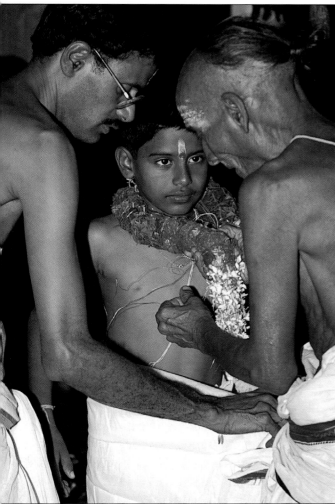

**B** Receiving the sacred thread marks the beginning of a Hindu boy's spiritual education

## A Hindu prayer

This is one of the prayers said by the father during the sacred thread ceremony:

*Oh, my child, this sacred thread is purified and will lead you to a knowledge of the Absolute [God]. The natural source of the sacred thread is God himself and it is bestowed again and again for eternity. It gives long life and favours thoughts of God. This thread I put round you... May it enlighten your mind.*

 **Find the answers**

- What is the tenth samskara and when does it take place?
- What is the special knot in the sacred thread called?
- Which three debts are owed by every Hindu boy and how does the sacred thread remind him of them?

 **Learning about, learning from**

1 Imagine you are spending a holiday with a Hindu family. Using the information on these pages, write a letter home to your parents describing a sacred thread ceremony you have attended.

2 The sacred thread itself reminds the boy that he has a three-fold debt to repay. It is not difficult to see what his debts to God and to his parents might be, but what do you think he might owe his ancestors and the spiritual wise men?

3 Which ceremony would you like to take part in to mark the time when you become an adult? How important do you think it is to mark such an occasion?

 **Extra activity**

Many religions offer their followers a 'new start' in life. In Hinduism they are said to be 'twice-born', while Christians speak of being 'born again'.
a. What do these two phrases mean?
b. Why is it important for people to be offered a fresh start in life, with the 'slate wiped clean'?

# Amrit Sanskar

**A** It is open to Sikh young people to show commitment to their faith by becoming members of the Khalsa

In the Sikh religion, boys and girls can go through the Amrit Sanskar at any time from adolescence onwards. This ceremony was first introduced by Guru Gobind Singh, the tenth and last Guru, on 30 March 1699 CE. This event is now commemorated in the major Sikh festival of **Baisakhi**.

## The ceremony

Standing with arms folded in front of five Khalsa members called the **panj piares** ('five beloved ones'), the ceremony involves the person asking to be admitted into the Sikh brotherhood of believers. Not all Sikhs join this fellowship, but the decision to do so shows a high level of commitment to the Sikh faith.

Each of the five Khalsa members present wears a yellow tunic with a sash. They conduct the service and begin by reciting the duties of each member of the Khalsa. These include:

- getting up early, bathing and saying morning prayers
- saying the evening prayers before going to bed at night
- saying the Ardas prayer regularly
- living by the rules of the Sikh religion
- wearing the **Five Ks** – the **kesh, kangha, kirpan, kachs** and **kara**
- avoiding all alcohol, tobacco and sexual relations outside marriage
- working hard and honestly to provide for the needs of their family
- treating all Sikhs honestly as brothers and sisters
- giving away 10 per cent of income to the poor.

The main part of the ceremony, which takes several hours, is the drinking of a nectar called amrit. This is a mixture of water and sugar crystals, which is mixed in a silver bowl using a sword by each of the panj piares. As they do so, they recite a passage from the Guru Granth Sahib. The mixture is then sprinkled on the hair and eyes of each candidate. From this moment onwards, they carry the full responsibility of belonging to the Khalsa. The ceremony ends, as in the case of all Sikh religious services, with the distribution of karah parshad to everyone who is present. Men initiated into the Khalsa take on a new name, either as a middle name or surname.

## Breaking the vows

At the Amrit ceremony a Sikh takes some important vows which they may fail to keep at some time. If this happens, they must confess their failure in front of the congregation in the gurdwara and ask for forgiveness. The community will then decide what form of punishment is most appropriate. This is called tankha (penance). After the penance has been carried out, the person is fully restored to the Sikh community but they have to undergo the Amrit Sanskar again. It is hoped that he or she will learn from their experience and will not fail in the same way again. It is also hoped that by such discipline the purity of the Sikh brotherhood is maintained.

**B** Karah parshad is distributed at the end of every important Sikh ceremony, including Amrit Sanskar

## In the glossary

| | |
|---|---|
| Baisakhi | Kara |
| Five Ks | Kesh |
| Kachs | Kirpan |
| Kangha | Panj piares |

 **Find the answers**

- Who first introduced the Amrit Sanskar?
- Who conducts the ceremony?
- What is tankha?

 **Learning about, learning from**

1 Imagine you are a Sikh. Explain the importance of the vows that you took at your Amrit Sanskar to a schoolfriend who is not a Sikh.

2 **a.** Why is amrit is sprinkled on each worshipper's hair and eyes?
**b.** Make a list of the similarities between the Amrit ceremony (with its sprinkling of nectar) and either infant baptism or believer's baptism as practised by the Christian Church.

3 Imagine you are a reporter for a local newspaper. You have been sent to a gurdwara to write a report on a Sikh Amrit ceremony. Write your article, beginning with the words: 'Last Tuesday in the local gurdwara...' Avoid simply reporting the facts – explain something of the Sikh faith and the meaning of the ceremony. Illustrate your report to make it more interesting.

 **Extra activity**

Why does a person who breaks their Amrit vows have to ask for forgiveness in front of the whole Sikh congregation?

# 5 Marriage

## Introduction

Marriage is the union between a man and a woman as husband and wife, neither of whom is married to someone else at the time. The only possible exception to this is in Islam, where the Qur'an allows a man to have up to four wives at the same time. In practice, however, this is very much the exception in Muslim communities. Whatever the religion, marriage is always a very special event.

### A legal agreement

Every marriage in Britain must be solemnised (made legal) in the presence of an official called a registrar. In most church weddings, the priest or minister who conducts the service also acts as the registrar. After the religious service, the couple, with two witnesses, must sign the register. When they do so they are legally married and given a certificate as legal proof.

The couple marrying can decide whether or not they want their wedding to have a religious significance. Slightly less than half of all weddings in Britain are carried out in places of worship; the rest are performed in registry offices and other buildings, such as hotels, which are licensed for the purpose. Many couples marrying in a place of worship do so because they wish the ceremony to take place 'in the presence of God'.

The most serious aspect of a wedding is the vows that the couple make to each other, promising to love and look after each other until one of them dies. Although most religions now accept divorce, they do so only as a last resort, stressing that couples should aim for a lifelong partnership.

### Arranged marriages

The practice of parents arranging the marriage of their children is still common in many religions. It is argued that this uses the experience and wisdom of two families, so giving the couple the best possible chance of enjoying future happiness. In Hinduism and Sikhism, in particular, marriage is seen as much more than the decision of two people to become husband and wife. It brings together and unites two families, as well as having a great influence on the religious life of the community.

### Celebrations

Celebrating is an essential part of a wedding in any part of the world. The marriage celebrations are usually very colourful and joyful, and may well go on for a long time. Hindu weddings, for example, often last for three days, with the couple becoming legally married only towards the end of the festivities.

# In this unit

## In this unit you will read about the following:

- Christian weddings, in which the giving and receiving of promises forms the heart of the service. A ring is given to the bride, or exchanged between bride and groom, as a symbol of their undying love for one another.

- Jewish weddings, in which the groom signs the **ketubah** (contract) committing him to honour his wife at all times. Jewish marriages can take place at home or in the synagogue.

- A Muslim wedding does not have to take place in a mosque because it is a civil, and not a religious, ceremony. The Qur'an plays a very important part in the service.

- A Hindu wedding always takes place around a sacred fire, leading up to the moment when the couple take seven steps around the fire bound together by a white cord.

- There is no marriage contract exchanged between the couple in a Sikh wedding. Instead it is enough that the wedding has taken place in front of the Guru Granth Sahib, the holy book that symbolises the presence of God.

- Marriage marks the beginning of an important stage in the life of a Buddhist. One school of Buddhism, however, believes that marriage symbolises the turning away from spiritual to material goals. The best that a married person can hope for is to be reborn at a higher level in the next life.

## In the glossary

Ketubah

55

# Christian weddings

Like the other religions, Christianity sets a very high value on marriage. In the Bible the relationship between a husband and wife is compared to the bond between Christ and the Church. Jesus taught that this relationship should be loving and permanent (see the box on the next page).

## Church traditions

Most weddings are traditional. In the Church of England the process begins when the banns (the public announcement of a forthcoming wedding) are read out in the parish of the man and woman on three successive Sundays. Although there are plans to omit these banns in future, they have traditionally provided an opportunity for a person to speak out against the wedding going ahead.

Brides in church traditionally wear white as a sign of their purity and virginity. During the service the bride is 'given away' by her father or a close male relative. This custom goes back to the time when daughters were considered to be their father's property. The groom has a best man to assist him during the ceremony. In the Orthodox Church, it is the tradition for godparents to play a part in the wedding of their godchild.

## The wedding service

During the wedding service, the priest explains to the couple just how the Church sees marriage. He says to them:

> Marriage is a way of life that all should honour, and it must not be taken lightly, carelessly or selfishly but reverently, responsibly and after serious thought.

At this point the couple exchange their vows. They promise to love and cherish each other:

> for better, for worse, for richer, for poorer, in sickness and in health... till death us do part according to God's holy law.

The groom places a wedding ring on the fourth finger of the bride's left hand and she may do the same to him. The ring, without beginning or end, is a symbol of their undying love for each other. They then say:

> With my body I honour you, all that I am I give to you, and all that I have I share with you.

The priest then tells the couple:

> I therefore proclaim that you are husband and wife. That which God has joined together, let no man divide.

**A** A wedding ring is a symbol of a couple's unending love for each other

**B** A Christian wedding involves the commitment of a man and a woman to each other in the sight of God

# From the Church of England wedding service

In the Church of England wedding service the priest tells the bride and groom:

*Marriage is given that a husband and wife may comfort and help each other, living faithfully together in need and plenty, in sorrow and in joy. It is given that with delight and tenderness, they may know each other in love and through the joy of their bodily union may strengthen the union of their hearts and lives. It is given that they may have children and be blessed in caring for them, and bring them up in accordance with God's will, to his praise and glory.*

 **Find the answers**

- What are the banns?
- Who is the best man?
- What is a vow?

 **Learning about, learning from**

**1 a.** In the quotation from the Church of England wedding ceremony in the box, three reasons are given for marriage. What are they?

**b.** Do you think the reasons have been placed in this order to indicate their importance? If so, do you agree with the order?

**2** What promises do a man and a woman make to each other during the wedding service?

**3 a.** Describe two vows in the Christian wedding service.

**b.** In Britain today more than one in three marriages ends in divorce. Do you think couples should renew their marriage vows regularly? Explain the reasons behind your answer.

 **Extra activity**

Bearing in mind the wedding vows made in church, do you think someone who has been married in a church should be allowed, after divorce, to remarry someone else in church? Should the Christian Church allow them to marry a second time or not? Explain your answer.

# Jewish weddings

The Talmud, one of the Jewish holy books, says that without a wife a man is incomplete. It advises all men to study first and then to marry. If, however, a man cannot wait to marry, he can reverse the order!

## A gift from God

In the Jewish faith, marriage is seen as a gift from God, bringing great joy and peace. A Jewish wedding is an opportunity for the whole community to come together and join in the joy of the couple. A new Jewish home is set up, which will, it is hoped, be blessed before long with the gift of children.

Although most Jewish weddings take place in the synagogue, they can take place anywhere, even outdoors. It is traditional for the marriage to take place on a Tuesday because in creating the world God said twice that the third day of creation, a Tuesday, was good. In practice, though, a Jewish wedding can take place on any day of the week except the Sabbath Day or a festival day. For the marriage to take place in a synagogue, both the man and the woman must be Jewish.

## Before the service

Before the service takes place, the groom signs the ketubah (wedding contract). This is for the bride's benefit and in it he states:

> I faithfully promise that I will be a true husband unto thee. I will honour and cherish thee. I will work for thee. I will protect and support thee.

The bridegroom and his father than stand beneath the huppah (wedding canopy), waiting for the arrival of the bride. The whole service is conducted beneath the canopy as it symbolises togetherness and the home that the couple are about to set up together. It has open sides to remind them that they are part of the wider Jewish community. The groom wears a skull-cap on his head for the ceremony. The bride is dressed in a long white dress with a veil.

## The wedding service

The service begins with two blessings. The bride and groom share a goblet of wine before the groom places a plain gold ring on the bride's finger. As he does so, he says in Hebrew:

> Behold thou art consecrated to me by this ring according to the Law of Moses and Israel.

After the ketubah has been read aloud, seven blessings are pronounced over the couple and another glass of wine is drunk. The groom then crushes an empty wine glass beneath his feet. This important symbolic act reminds everyone of the destruction of the Temple in Jerusalem in 586 BCE and the suffering of the Jews

**A** The ketubah is the document that outlines a groom's responsibilities towards his bride through the ages. It also reminds the couple that their married life ahead will be full of good and bad times.

Before the service ends, everyone shouts out 'Mazel Tov' ('good luck') to the couple. Then all the guests are invited to a wedding feast to celebrate what is an important and happy event for everyone.

**B** The wedding canopy, or huppah, symbolises the new home that a Jewish couple will set up together

## From the Talmud

One of the Jewish holy books, the Talmud, states:
*Your wife has been given to you in order that you might realise with her life's great plan.*

## Find the answers

- Why have Jewish weddings traditionally been held on Tuesdays?
- What is the ketubah?
- What does the crushing of a wine glass beneath the groom's foot symbolise?

## Learning about, learning from

1 Make a list of the different symbols associated with a Jewish wedding. Explain what two of them mean.

2 Compare the main promises made in the ketubah with those in the Christian wedding service (pages 56 and 57). What similarities are there?

3 The Talmud says that without a wife a man is incomplete.
   a. What do you think this statement means?
   b. Do you agree or disagree? Explain your answer.
   c. Is a woman incomplete without a husband? Explain your answer.

## Extra activity

Most religions stress the importance of two people from the same faith marrying each other.
a. Think of two reasons why this is thought to be important.
b. Are there any problems that could arise if two people from different faiths married each other?

# Muslim weddings

In most Muslim countries, the marriage of a man and a woman is arranged by their parents. This does not mean, however, that the couple have no say in the matter. They are involved and consulted about the choice. A forced marriage is not a real marriage. However, as a Muslim wedding involves the uniting of two families, it is thought only right that the families should be involved in the process.

## The marriage contract

In Islam the two people who sign the marriage contract must be making a free decision to marry each other. The Qur'an makes it clear that no pressure must be put on them. Before the marriage can go ahead, the man must present the woman with a dowry (wedding gift), which becomes her property. The first part is paid over immediately, but the second part is paid only if the husband requests a divorce. Muhammad taught that a woman's family should not ask for a very large dowry, but neither should they settle for nothing. It is necessary as a safeguard that the woman will not end up in poverty. The exact value of the dowry is settled through negotiations between the two families.

At every Muslim marriage there must be at least two witnesses, one of whom must be a man. Couples are thought more likely to keep to the terms of their wedding contract if it is made in public in front of witnesses.

## The wedding service

Although in Britain it is convenient for most Muslim wedding services to take place in a mosque, they do not have to be held in a place of worship. During the service the man and the woman promise each other that:

> [they will do] their best to base their marriage on the teaching of God, to make it a relationship of mutual love, mercy, peace, faithfulness and co-operation.

The recital of verses from the Qur'an forms an important part of a Muslim wedding service. The most likely reading from the holy book is the one given in the box on the next page, which is taken from a chapter of the Qur'an called 'The Women'.

After a talk from the **imam** on the responsibilities that husbands and wives have to each other, the couple exchange rings. The one given to the man can be of any metal except gold. The guests congratulate the couple by saying 'Baarakal-Lahu Lakum wa Baaraka Alaykum' ('May God bless you and send His blessing on you').

**A** A Muslim wedding involves the coming together of two families, not just the uniting of one couple

The ceremony is followed by a big feast, which can go on for as long as seven days. In some Muslim countries the bride, wearing a very elaborate costume, is carried in a chair by four women away from the wedding celebrations to the bedroom.

**B** In a Muslim wedding the couple promise to be faithful to each other and to Allah

## From the Qur'an

This is what the Qur'an says about marriage:

*And among His signs is this, that He created for your mates from among yourselves, that ye may dwell in tranquility with them. And He has put love and mercy between your hearts.*

### Find the answers

- What do the man and the woman agree before a Muslim marriage takes place?

- What is a dowry?

- Why are witnesses important at a Muslim marriage?

### Learning about, learning from

1 Describe what happens during a Muslim wedding service, and draw pictures to illustrate your description.

2 Read the quotation from the Qur'an in the box.
   a. Which two qualities does Allah give to those who marry?
   b. How does the Qur'an expect two married people to live together?

### Extra activity

In most religions, marriage is a holy occasion when two people make promises in the presence of God. While it does have religious significance to Muslims, the most commonly held Muslim view is that marriage is largely a social event. Do you think that marriage is a religious or a social event?

### In the glossary

Imam

# Hindu weddings

In Hinduism marriage is the thirteenth of the sixteen samskaras. The ceremony can take place in the temple or at the bride's home. The actual date for the wedding is fixed by the priest after he has consulted the horoscopes of the couple. Great care is taken to prepare a Hindu bride for her wedding. After she has taken a bath, her hands and the soles of her feet are decorated in intricate patterns with henna (orange plant dye). Ointment is rubbed all over her body. A mixture of ghee (clarified butter), camphor and herbs is put around the eyes. She then puts on a red sari for the ceremony.

## The wedding service

At the beginning of the wedding service, worship is offered to Ganesha, the elephant god. The ceremony then continues under a special canopy, which is decorated with tinsel and lights. When the priest arrives to conduct the ceremony, his feet are washed and he is honoured highly. His first act is to light the holy fire as a sign that the god Agni is present.

A white cord is then attached to the shoulders of the couple and they take seven steps around the sacred fire. Each of these steps has a special significance – the couple hope for food, strength, increasing wealth, happiness and good fortune, children, enjoyment of the seasons and everlasting friendship. At each step the couple pause to make their promises to each other. The bride also places her foot on a stone as a sign that she is to remain as stable as that stone throughout her married life. She promises to love her husband and his family as she does her own.

Flower petals and garlands are then thrown over the couple before the guests come forward with gifts. Prayers for good fortune and peace bring the service to a close. After the sun has set, however, the couple pledge their faithfulness to each other once more as they stand gazing at the Pole Star.

## The Hindu household

The Hindu wife is called ardhangani ('the half of my body'). Within the home she is in control of the family and takes responsibility for arranging all the worship that takes place there. The wife

A The preparation of a Hindu bride for her wedding involves many members of the family

has the duty of saying prayers in front of the family's shrine and making the correct food offerings. The husband plays no part in running a Hindu household. All the Hindu holy books stress that a marriage should never be broken. The one exception is where a Hindu wife agrees to divorce her husband because she cannot have any children. Every Hindu wife believes she has a duty to produce children, especially sons, so that the family name of her husband will be carried on.

**B** A Hindu wedding is conducted in the presence of Agni, the god of fire

## From the wedding service

As the couple take seven steps around the sacred fire, the man says to the woman:
*With utmost love to each other may we walk together... May we make our minds united, of the same vows and of the same thoughts. I am the wind and you are the melody. I am the melody and you are the words.*

## Find the answers

- How does the priest set the date for a Hindu wedding?
- The sacred fire is a symbol for which god?
- How many times do the wedding couple walk around the sacred fire?

## Learning about, learning from

1 Describe four things that a Hindu bride does to prepare herself for marriage.

2 **a.** Describe three symbolic actions that are performed in a Hindu marriage and explain what they mean.
**b.** Why are these actions performed?

3 Read the quotation from the wedding ceremony in the box. What does the following phrase mean? 'I am the wind and you are the melody. I am the melody and you are the words'.

## Extra activity

It is customary for the couple to end their wedding day by looking up at the Pole Star and promising to be faithful to each other. The Pole Star was often used by travellers and sailors to navigate by. Can you think of any qualities that the Pole Star might have which a couple may wish for in their married life together?

# Sikh weddings

**A** In Sikhism, marriage is an important spiritual journey which lasts for the remainder of a couple's life

Marriage is a part of spiritual development and growth for all Sikhs. They try to make sure that they marry a fellow Sikh because that alone will be beneficial to them. Marriage is an important spiritual journey which draws the soul closer to God. As the couple help each other to draw closer to God, so they find themselves being drawn closer to each other as well.

## The wedding service

A Sikh wedding is usually arranged by the parents and is called **anand karaj** ('the ceremony of bliss'). Before the wedding, the fathers of the bride and groom, the grandfathers and the mothers' brothers all meet together. This first meeting is symbolically very important because it recognises that marriage in the Sikh community is as much the uniting of two families as it is the coming together of two people.

The ceremony normally takes place early in the morning. The bride is usually dressed in a red shalwar kameez (the traditional tunic and trousers) embroidered with gold thread, although other colours may be worn. The only colour not permitted is white because that is the colour of mourning. The groom wears a suit with a red or pink turban. The couple sit cross-legged on the floor of the gurdwara in front of the Guru Granth Sahib. The service begins with the granthi reminding the couple of the responsibilities of marriage. He asks them whether they are prepared to accept these responsibilities. They show that they are by bowing low in front of the holy book.

Garlands of flowers are placed around the necks of the bride and groom. A cotton scarf is draped over the groom's shoulder, with his bride being given one end to hold. For the rest of the service they are joined together in this way. It is a symbol which underlines that, from now on, all their decisions will be made jointly.

A marriage hymn is read before the couple walk slowly around the Guru Granth Sahib, the groom leading the way. The bride, holding the scarf, keeps in step and the hymn is repeated by the musicians. When the couple reach the front of the holy book, they bow before sitting down. In all, the couple walk around the Guru Granth Sahib four times in a clockwise direction. At the end of the service the bride's mother presents the groom with a piece of sweetmeat. This shows that he is now accepted as a full member of her family.

## No contract

Unlike many other world religions, there is no marriage contract to be signed by the bride and groom at a Sikh wedding. They have made their promises to God – in the form of the Guru Granth Sahib – and to each other. This is considered enough and no written contract is required. By making promises in the presence of God to love and take care of each other, they have a duty to keep them for the rest of their lives. Sikhs believe if they fail to do so it would have made no difference if they had entered into a written contract.

**B** A Sikh marriage is the uniting of two families and not just two people

## In the glossary

Anand karaj

## The importance of women

This extract from the Guru Granth Sahib speaks about the importance of women:
*It is by women that we are conceived... and from them we are born... it is the women who keep the race going... Why should women be thought inferior when they give birth to great men?*

 **Find the answers**

- Why do the male members of both families meet before the wedding?

- How many times do the couple walk around the Guru Granth Sahib?

- Why does the bride's mother give the groom a piece of sweetmeat?

 **Learning about, learning from**

1 Choose four important parts of the Sikh wedding service. Draw pictures to illustrate them and write a short description underneath each drawing.

2 Why is a Sikh wedding ceremony always carried out in front of the Guru Granth Sahib?

3 The bride and the groom are joined together for much of the Sikh wedding service by a scarf. What do you think this is saying about their future marriage?

 **Extra activity**

What does the Sikh name for the wedding service tell you about the attitude of this religion to marriage?

# Buddhist weddings

Marriage is very important in Buddhism, but it does not have any particular religious significance. By marrying, a man and a woman are beginning the life of a householder and these are very respected figures in Buddhist society. The **sangha** (the community of **monks**) depends on them for their food and clothing. In **Theravada Buddhism**, however, it is thought that no one can reach spiritual enlightenment through being a householder. This is a view which is not shared in **Mahayana Buddhism**.

## Marriage in Theravada Buddhism

Theravada Buddhism teaches that when a person marries they have set themselves worldly (non-spiritual) goals. There are many things that can distract a householder from following the path to enlightenment. By becoming a householder, the best that a person can

hope for is to be reborn at a higher level in the next life. For this reason there is no marriage service in Theravada Buddhism. Theravada Buddhists are free to marry according to the customs of the country in which they live.

On the morning of their marriage, monks are invited into the bride's home for a special feast. They recite special texts from the holy books to protect the bride and groom from danger. They then return to the **monastery** before the wedding ceremony begins – they do not play any part in the service itself.

## Marriage in Mahayana Buddhism

In Mahayana Buddhism, the teaching is that householders can reach enlightenment. In Tibet and Japan some Buddhist priests are married. The Mahayana wedding ceremony is usually carried out in the home by one of the bride's male relatives. The couple stand on a platform with the thumbs of their right hands or their right wrists tied together. This is a symbol of their new unity as husband and wife. They are now as one. The couple exchange rings and repeat promises that they will love and respect each other throughout their married life together.

Often a monk comes to a Mahayana wedding to read some holy texts. It is very important that the couple should hear the teachings of the **Buddha** on marriage. Alternatively, the couple may spend some time in a monastery listening to the monks reciting the texts. They are reminded that the Buddha himself had a wife and son before he went to find enlightenment. He taught that a man must honour and respect his wife and defer to her in all household matters. He must be

**A** A Buddhist marriage is a joyful occasion, but it does not have any particular religious significance

faithful to her at all times. The wife must perform her household responsibilities and show equal hospitality to her husband's and her own family. She, too, must be faithful at all times and take great care with the money her husband earns.

**B** The householder phase, through which almost all Buddhists pass, is not thought to be important on the way to enlightenment

## In the glossary

| | |
|---|---|
| Buddha | Monks |
| Mahayana Buddhism | Sangha |
| Monastery | Theravada Buddhism |

### Find the answers

- What is the sangha?
- Why is there no marriage service in Theravada Buddhism?
- Why do monks recite from the Buddhist scriptures before a Theravada wedding?

### Learning about, learning from

1 What part do monks play in:
   a. Theravada weddings?
   b. Mahayana weddings?

2 There is no marriage service in Theravada Buddhism because a person becomes a householder through marriage.
   a. Explain why the role of the householder, although very important, is not spiritually significant in Theravada Buddhism.
   b. When a person marries, what kind of things are likely to take up their mind instead of the search for spiritual enlightenment?
   c. Make a list of ten material things that might occupy the mind of someone who is married.

### Extra activity

Do you think that someone who marries is necessarily unable to pursue a spiritual way of life as Theravada Buddhism suggests? Explain your answer.

# 6 Suffering

# Introduction

Suffering is the experience of pain. The pain can be physical (in the body) or mental (in the mind). Some pain is good and necessary. It might tell us that something serious is wrong. It can be a warning sign. A toothache, for example, might indicate that an abscess is forming below the gum. If you ignore the warning sign, the consequences could be serious.

Yet much pain experienced in the world is not of this 'helpful' kind: young babies suffering malnutrition and dying before their first birthday; a mother and father dying in a car crash and leaving two young children without parents; children being born with disabilities that will stay with them for the rest of their lives. Then there are 'natural' disasters, such as floods, earthquakes and tornadoes, which destroy whole communities and shatter lives. There is so much suffering in today's world.

## Religion and suffering

The suffering in the world has always been of the greatest concern to all the world's religions. Indeed, one of them – Buddhism – was born out of the need to find an answer to the problem of suffering. All the other faiths needed to come to terms with the fact that they believe, to a greater or lesser extent, in a loving God who created the world and all forms of life. Why is there suffering in a world created by a loving God? Surely God would want to stop suffering? Religious people also believe in a God whose power and authority reach to the furthest ends of the earth. His power is unlimited. Surely, then, this God is able to end the suffering in the world?

Suffering, however, continues. For many religious believers, such as some of those who wrote in the Old Testament, life seemed to be almost without any meaning. Humans are born, spend barely a few decades on earth, and are then blown away like dust in the wind. During their short lifespan they have much suffering to cope with. This is the problem that most of the world's holy books tackle in their own way. They try to find a meaning and a purpose to an existence which often seems to have little purpose. Trying to make sense of life is probably the most important task a religion undertakes, and that includes making sense of suffering.

# In this unit

## In this unit you will read about the following:

- Christians and suffering. Christians believe that the answer to suffering is to be found in following the example of Jesus. Life and resurrection come out of suffering and death.

- Jews and suffering. Jews have suffered much but they have continued to believe in a God who loves and cares for them.

- Muslims and suffering. Muslims believe that Allah has absolute power over the whole of creation. Suffering is used by Allah to punish people for their sin and also to test their faith.

- Hindus and suffering. Hindus look to a person's past sins in previous lives to explain their suffering now.

- Sikhs and suffering. Sikhs believe that suffering is a mystery but that faith in God enables them to accept pleasure and pain in the same spirit of trust.

- Buddhists and suffering. Buddhists believe that suffering can take many forms and that, through many rebirths, its effects can be overcome. It is not finally overcome, however, until a state of enlightenment has been reached.

## From the Talmud

This is from the Talmud, a Jewish holy book:

*When the Holy One, blessed be he, reflects that his children are plunged in distress among the nations of the world, he drops two tears into the Great Sea, and the sound is heard from one end of the world to the other.*

# Christians and suffering

To all believers in God, suffering presents a very big problem and Christians are no exception. How can a God who is all-loving and all-powerful allow suffering? If God is all-powerful, He should be able to prevent suffering. If God is all-loving, He should want to prevent suffering.

## Christians and suffering

Over the centuries, Christians have come forward with many possible explanations for suffering. Here are some of them:

- Suffering comes from sin. People are naturally selfish and self-centred. Selfish behaviour always hurts other people. Much of the suffering in the world is brought about by people acting in a selfish way.
- Suffering is part and parcel of human life. In fact, life would be much poorer without it. Through suffering, people learn that they have deep inner resources. Suffering teaches them patience and courage. It gives them something to fight against, which is very important.
- Suffering shows that people have free will. They are always free to choose between right and wrong, good and evil. Without such free will, they would be little more than machines. When people misuse their free will and hurt others, they are acting out of ignorance. Remove the ignorance and the world could be free of famine, cruelty, torture, pollution and racism, among other things.
- God suffers alongside humans when they suffer.

Christians trying to understand what suffering is all about look to Jesus and his suffering. He was the Son of God, yet he was tortured and put to death. Christians believe he rose from the dead, bringing hope and light out of death and despair. This gives them reason to look beyond the grave to heaven, when sickness and suffering will be no more.

## Helping those who suffer

Christians believe they should not simply accept the suffering in the world. Over the centuries, they have been active in helping those who suffer. They have done this mainly in two ways:

- By praying for them. Some people within the Church have been thought to have the 'gift of healing'. In the Roman Catholic Church, one of the seven sacraments has been that of anointing the sick with oil and asking for God to heal them. In recent years this sacrament has been given to anyone who needs to be healed, not just to those who are dying.
- By serving them. Many Christians have devoted themselves to serving others in need. They have worked in hospitals and hospices, and with organisations taking food and medical care to the poor and needy.

**A** The Christian attitude to suffering is greatly affected by what happened to Jesus on the cross

**B** Just as Jesus rose from the dead, so Christians believe that resurrection lies beyond suffering and death

## Love one another

Towards the end of his life, Jesus gave his followers a new commandment:

*I give you a new commandment: love one another as I have loved you.*

 **Find the answers**

- Who do Christians look to when they try to understand suffering?

- How many sacraments are used by the Roman Catholic Church?

- What do Roman Catholic priests do as they pray for people to be healed from their suffering?

 **Learning about, learning from**

**1** Why does suffering create problems for people who believe in God?

**2** Describe two answers that Christians give to the problem of suffering. Do you think they make sense?

**3** Some people say we learn far more about ourselves through pain and suffering than in any other way.
  **a.** What do you think pain and suffering might teach us?
  **b.** Are these lessons that we could not learn in any other way?

 **Extra activity**

**a.** Make a list of five kinds of suffering in the modern world.
**b.** How many of the things on your list could be avoided if people began to learn more about themselves and the needs of others?

# Jews and suffering

Jews believe that God is both good and all-powerful. This leads them to ask the question: Why do innocent people suffer? Why is a child born with an incurable illness that will cut his or her life short? Why do some people suffer throughout their lives and others do not? Why did God allow six million Jews to be murdered in the **Holocaust** during the Second World War?

There are no simple answers to these questions. Only the prophets, whose writings are found in the Jewish scriptures, were told by God the reasons for particular disasters. The **rabbis** and other Jewish leaders could not begin to understand the reasons for suffering, but they did work out ways of accepting it. These were often based on stories in the scriptures.

## Suffering

The scriptures tell us many stories of Jews who have come through suffering. Joseph was sold into slavery by his 11 brothers, Ruth was a young widow and very poor, King David lost his baby son, and the Book of Job is all about suffering.

It tells the story of a man who lost his family and home, enduring great pain and yet never losing his faith in God. The Jewish people spent over 400 years in Egyptian slavery and yet they managed to keep their faith.

Stories like these help Jews today to accept, and to understand, suffering. From them, Jews learn that such suffering may be a test of human faith sent as a punishment by God, or a reminder to people of the agreement made by Abraham that the Jews would keep God's laws. Suffering does not just happen. Jews believe God makes suffering happen. Because suffering comes from God, there must always be a reason for it. That reason, though, may not be obvious. When suffering appears to be meaningless, then is the time to trust in God.

The rabbis of old also taught something else about suffering. Suffering shows that each member of the human race is responsible for everyone else. It is not only the wicked who suffer. Often it is the good and righteous who suffer most. Sometimes the good suffer for the wicked. Suffering can refine a person's character. It teaches people to be more humble and patient. It reminds people that life is short.

At the same time, every effort should be made to relieve suffering. It is a religious duty to look after and visit the sick. The poor must be provided for and the bereaved must be comforted. Many Jewish organisations exist to bring comfort and help to those in need.

**A** The Yad Vashem memorial is a stark reminder of the millions of Jews who died in the Second World War

**B** The suffering of millions of Jews in the Second World War caused many people to doubt, or to give up, their faith in God

## A Jewish story

*The Talmud tells the story of a rabbi who wanted to see someone who had earned a place in heaven. He was shown two men in the market place. He asked: 'What is your job?' They replied: 'We are clowns. We try to lift people out of their sadness.'*

## In the glossary

Holocaust          Rabbis

 **Find the answers**

- Which group of people were given explanations for particular disasters by God?

- Which book in the Jewish scriptures is all about the problem of suffering?

- Where do Jews believe suffering comes from?

 **Learning about, learning from**

**1** Make a list of the different ways in which Jews try to understand and explain the existence of suffering.

**2 a.** Why do Jews today have a particular interest in understanding suffering?
**b.** Many people find it difficult to believe that God controls everything. Why do you think this is?

**3** What do you think about the different explanations that Judaism offers to explain suffering? In your opinion, do any of them offer an explanation that satisfies you?

### Extra activity

There is a saying in the Jewish scriptures which says: 'Not to have known suffering is not to be truly human.' What do you think this means?

# Muslims and suffering

Muslims believe that the Qur'an is the word of God. Its words carry Allah's authority in explaining how God expects all Muslims to live and behave. The holy book also explains the eternal destiny of all human beings. Muslims could not know these truths unless Allah had chosen to reveal them. In the Qur'an Allah is revealed as the one sovereign God who rules over the entire universe.

## Allah

To Muslims, God is present everywhere in the world. He knows everything about everyone and is all-powerful. He made everything, and there is nothing outside, over or beyond His authority. He has 99 known names and many of them stress His power and authority. He has all the power that goes with his sovereignity and majesty throughout the earth and the universe.

**A** The Qur'an teaches that all people are given freedom to act and so are responsible for the consequences of what they do, good and bad

Yet the actions of God constantly show his justice and mercy. He will treat the evil with justice and the righteous with mercy. Among his many names he is known as the Merciful and the Compassionate. The mercy of Allah is often emphasised in Muslim worship. It is traditional for a Muslim who is giving a speech or writing a letter to begin with the words: 'In the name of God, the Merciful and the Compassionate.'

## Understanding suffering

In the Qur'an it is revealed that all human beings are the creation of Allah. They must obey Him. Righteous people who would win the favour of Allah must submit themselves to Allah and His will. The very word 'Islam' means 'submission'. At the same time, humans can choose between right and wrong. They are responsible for the good and evil actions that they do. Allah, in His wisdom, has given them this freedom and so can hold them responsible for their actions.

The Qur'an teaches two important things about suffering:

- Suffering is a punishment for sin. God is absolutely just and righteous. He cannot overlook sin. Sin must always be punished by a God who is holy and righteous. That punishment takes place in this life through suffering. In the life to come it will result in the person being sent to hell.
- Suffering is a test of a person's faith. It is easy to believe in God when everything in life is going well. For most people, though, the real test of faith comes when life is not going so well. Allah sometimes brings suffering so that the strength of someone's faith may be tested.

**B** The Qur'an encourages Muslims to look at suffering as a test of their faith in Allah

## God rewards

The Qur'an tells us the following: *To God belongs whatsoever is in the heavens and whatsoever is in the earth, that He may recompense those who do evil for what they have done, and recompense those who have done good with the reward most fair.*

 **Find the answers**

- Which book carries Allah's authority?

- What are some of the names for Allah in the Qur'an?

- What does the word 'Islam' mean?

 **Learning about, learning from**

1 Make a list of the different things that Muslims believe about Allah.

2 Why can human beings be held responsible by Allah for their actions – both good and bad?

3 When asked about the reasons for suffering in the world, Muslims may give you two answers. What are they?

4 How do the beliefs that Muslims hold about Allah affect the way they look at suffering?

**Extra activity**

What thing is necessary for someone to be held fully responsible for their actions? Do you think this is true of everyone?

# Hindus and suffering

Hinduism teaches that some human beings are more inclined than others to commit sinful actions. These actions result in evil like adultery, theft, telling lies and murder. Causing injury or suffering to others are also evil actions. This tendency towards evil is explained by the law of karma.

**A** The plight of many Hindus is blamed on bad actions they have committed in a past life

## Karma and suffering

The law of karma is very important in Hinduism. It simply means that the soul cannot escape the consequences of its past actions. All suffering comes from the way people have behaved in the past. A soul's next existence is always determined by karma – the result of good and bad actions – in previous lives. Bad karma can be improved by good actions.

If any creature – bird, animal or human – experiences suffering, it is because of the bad karma that they carry from a past life. A good life is the result of good karma. A bad life, including suffering, is the result of bad karma. No one can blame God, or another human being, for the suffering they experience. It is simply the result of their past actions. They have only themselves to blame.

## Responding to suffering

To some Hindus, this teaching about suffering has led them to be uncaring about the suffering of others. If a person is suffering because of things they have done in the past, why feel sorry for them or try to help them? Suffering is, after all, a person's just reward for their own past sinful actions. In India, where four out of every five people are Hindus, millions of people suffer from a shortage of food, shelter and medical care. Animals, too, suffer from a lack of proper care. Millions of people die at a young age every year because of this. For many, this is simply the deserved result of bad karma.

To act like this, however, means ignoring other equally important Hindu teachings. Hinduism also teaches that the whole of creation is one. What happens to one part of creation also affects every other part. This means that one part of creation must love and care for another. If one part suffers, everyone else must help. Many Hindus accept that they are responsible for the care of others. Schools, colleges and hospitals are funded by Hindus because they care about the well-being of others. They help fellow Hindus to become better educated, self-sufficient and employed.

It is also possible that many Hindus are not really aware of the suffering of others. They worship individually or as a family, but not as a congregation. For this reason many Hindus do not see at first hand the suffering that others may experience.

**B** Hindus hope that their status in the next life will improve

## Krishna speaks

These words of the god Krishna are found in the **Bhagavad Gita**:
*The result of a virtuous [good] action is pure joy; actions done out of passion [bad actions] bring pain and suffering; ignorance arises from actions motivated by 'dark' [sinful] intentions.*

---

**In the glossary**

**Bhagavad Gita**

 **Find the answers**

- Which law in Hinduism states that a soul cannot escape the consequences of past actions?
- To whom is a Hindu responsible?
- Why may many Hindus not be aware of the suffering of others?

**Learning about, learning from**

**1 a.** Make a list of five actions that a Hindu would describe as 'sinful'.
**b.** What determines a soul's next existence?
**c.** If a person suffers, who is to blame?

**2 a.** Describe in no more than four sentences what karma is.
**b.** How is karma linked to suffering?

**3** How might Hindus in India explain the suffering that they see around them?

 **Extra activity**

How do you feel about the Hindu explanation of suffering?

# Sikhs and suffering

Suffering is real for Sikhs. They believe that every religious person must seek to rise above it. Much of the suffering that is in the world can be explained without any real difficulty. Sikhs believe that there are laws about how we should behave, which we ignore at our peril. These laws are the same whether we are rich or poor, educated or uneducated, wise or foolish. The consequences of breaking these laws can be very serious. As Guru Nanak said: 'Whoever will taste poison will die.'

## The mystery of suffering

The reason why many things happen in this life, both good and bad, can only remain a mystery to us. Guru Nanak taught his followers that the more they find out, the more there is to know. Suffering is a deep mystery that will never be solved. It is particularly puzzling why some people seem to suffer rarely while others have a much harder time. The only answer is 'God alone knows'. It may be unfair that the mugger escapes free while his victim is scarred for life, but God provides a spirit which is able to rise above the suffering. God does not *bring*

the suffering, but He does help us to deal with it. This is true of all 'innocent suffering'.

## Faith can overcome pain

The better a person comes to know God, the more they are willing to accept His will. This same person can accept the pleasure and the pain of life equally (see the box on the next page). The fifth Guru, Arjan, and the ninth Guru, Tegh Bahadur, suffered greatly at the hands of others. Both were able to accept what was happening as the will of God, and their faith was strengthened, not destroyed.

Faith, therefore, can overcome pain. Sikhs do not believe, however, that God causes people to suffer so that their faith may be tested or strengthened. This would be immoral. Humans can accept or reject God as they wish. God wants only those who are willing to serve Him. Sikhs do not believe that those who reject God and His love will be punished eternally. That, too, would be immoral. Much suffering in the world is inflicted by human beings on other human beings. It is foolish to try to blame God. Humans should be sensible enough not to bring suffering to others by what they do.

## The five evils

Sikhs believe that everything, even evil, comes from God. For example, God has put plants in the world, some of which are poisonous and some of which are medicinal. In a similar way, God allows us to choose to live good or bad lives. We have to make the choice. We cannot blame God if we suffer because we have made the wrong choice. Sikhs believe that there are five evils in this world: lust, anger, greed, attachment and pride.

**A** Suffering to Sikhs is the result of breaking the laws which govern life

 To Sikhs, suffering is a deep mystery

## From Guru Nanak

Guru Nanak taught that:
*Both poison and nectar are made by the Creator; both fruits grow on the tree of this world. Everything is in the Creator's hands. We are given to eat as much of them as it pleases God to give us.*

### Find the answers

- What do Sikhs see as being a deep mystery?
- Which two Gurus are a great example to Sikhs who suffer?
- What are the five evils?

 **Learning about, learning from**

1  What was Guru Nanak trying to teach his followers when he said: 'Whoever will taste poison will die'?

2  Think of one example of 'innocent suffering'. How do you think a Sikh might explain it?

3  Why do Sikhs believe that lust, anger, greed, attachment and pride are particularly evil? Explain your answer.

4  Describe two things that Sikhs believe to be immoral.

### Extra activity

Read the quotation by Guru Nanak in the box.
a. Rewrite the extract in your own words.
b. Do you think it is surprising to read that God creates everything, both good and bad? If so, what is surprising about it?

# Buddhists and suffering

The truth about suffering is the point from which all the teaching of Buddhism begins. It was the discovery of this truth that led Siddhartha Gotama to become the Buddha (the Enlightened One). The Buddha realised that the cycle of birth, life death and rebirth (**samsara**) offers no hope for the end of suffering. All human beings are born in suffering to live and die in suffering. The only hope lies in the ability to break out of this cycle.

Buddhists believe that there are eight kinds of suffering in samsara, none of which can be avoided:

- The suffering of being born.
- The suffering of growing old.
- The suffering brought about by sickness.
- The suffering of death.
- The suffering of being separated from loved ones or objects.
- The suffering brought on by unpleasant experiences.
- The suffering of being denied what we want.

- The suffering caused by our own delusions and karma.

## Ignorance and evil

The Buddha taught that all suffering is caused by ignorance. Although a person's actions hurt others, they are the ones who suffer most. The great discovery of the Buddha was that all suffering begins, and has its cure, in the mind (see the box on the next page). To overcome suffering, people must realise that harmful actions do not bring happiness. Once they accept this, they can train their mind to overcome the obstacles to happiness. The first step to remove ignorance is to accept the first of the **Four Noble Truths** (**dukkha**).

## Seeking happiness

Buddhists believe that people, through ignorance, seek pleasure in this life. They do this because of their karma. True happiness, though, is to be found in a deliverance from samsara. This does not mean that Buddhists should always be miserable. Sometimes life brings many pleasures. When it does, a Buddhist should always enjoy them to the full. True happiness, and relief from suffering, is not to be found, however, in the pleasures the world gives. They will lead to more suffering not away from it. Happiness is an inner experience. It is a matter of discovering and enjoying what is already inside each of us. To discover this secret means that we will not be always striving for what lies just beyond our reach. When we discover this, we will exchange a lie for the truth.

**A** Buddhists believe there is no hope for an end to suffering until the cycle of birth, life, death and rebirth is broken

**B** Buddhists believe that suffering is caused by ignorance of the way that suffering can be ended

## False pleasure

A Buddhist teacher wrote:
*Using our present rebirth only to enjoy samsaric pleasures is like being a dumb animal that eats the grass at the edge of the cliff, in constant danger of falling off.*

## In the glossary

Dukkha                     Samsara
Four Noble Truths

 **Find the answers**

- Who discovered the truth about suffering?

- What is samsara?

- How many kinds of suffering are recognised by Buddhists?

**Learning about, learning from**

**1** Look at the eight kinds of suffering recognised by Buddhists. Describe the kind of suffering that is involved in two of them.

**2** Write down three pleasures in life which do not bring suffering or pain to others. These must be pleasures which are good in themselves and so could not be used to harm others.

**3** Buddhists believe that happiness is an inner state of mind which does not depend on anything else.
   **a.** What do you think happiness is?
   **b.** Make a list of five things that make you very happy.

 **Extra activity**

A Buddhist master wrote: 'The village I reach at last, deeper than the deep mountains. What joy the capital where I have always lived.' This sums up the Buddhist attitude to happiness. What point is the master making?

# 7 Death and beyond

## Introduction

Death both fascinates and repels us. It is probably the last great taboo in most societies, particularly those in the Western world. People are generally embarrassed to talk about it. We have invented a series of phrases to help us to talk about it comfortably, such as 'passed away' and 'passed over'. We employ other people to deal with the practical aspects of death soon after it has happened. Shortly after death, the undertaker or funeral director takes over.

In many societies, however, there is a much closer contact with death. In Orthodox Christian services, for example, the coffin is left open for people to pay their last respects until the body is buried. In Judaism, members of the Jewish community make sure the body is accompanied until the last moment. In Islam, the body, in a simple linen shroud, is laid so that it touches the earth. Hindus burn the dead body in full view of everyone and then deal sensitively with the ashes that remain.

Funerals are important religious services because they reflect the beliefs that the different religions hold about death and life after death. These beliefs can be divided into two groups:

- Those who believe that each person has only one life, but that the soul survives death to live on in either heaven or hell for eternity. This is the basic belief held by Christians, Jews and Muslims. At some time after death, the soul has to face the judgement of God. Religions differ as to whether this judgement happens soon after a person's death or at some future time.

- Those who believe that the body dies but that the soul returns in another body. This belief is called **reincarnation**. With some differences, this belief is held by Hindus, Sikhs and Buddhists. All these religions teach that many rebirths are necessary before the soul enters what Buddhists call **nirvana**.

No one can be sure, of course, about what happens after death. It is perfectly possible that there is nothing but oblivion – no judgement to be faced and no endless rebirths. People who do not believe in God, often called 'humanists', believe that nothing survives after death except the memories of that person in the minds and hearts of the people who loved them.

# In this unit

## In this unit you will read about the following:

- The Christian approach to death combines great sadness with hope for the future. This hope is that the dead will be reunited with their loved ones in the next life. They will then spend eternity in the presence of God.

- The Jewish approach to death lays down guidelines about dealing with the dead body and the period of mourning that must follow death. Judaism is not clear in its teachings on life after death.

- Muslims are clear that death and the funeral that follows should be dealt with simply. After death comes the judgement of Allah, during which those destined for heaven are separated from those who will be sent to hell.

- Almost all Hindus are cremated after death. They believe that the soul leaves the body at death, seeking another body to live in.

- In the Sikh community, cremation is followed by a continual 48-hour reading of the Guru Granth Sahib. Sikhs believe that the body and soul separate at death, with the soul seeking another body. This continues to happen until the soul is reunited with God.

- Buddhism teaches that death is inevitable and that life is passing. Many rebirths are needed before enlightenment is reached and the soul enters nirvana.

## From the Jewish scriptures

One proverb in the Old Testament says that:

*A person's soul is like a candle lit by God.*

## In the glossary

Nirvana            Reincarnation

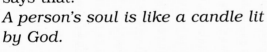

# Christian funerals

**A** Christians believe that the end of this life marks the beginning of eternal life

Christians believe strongly in life after death. This belief is reflected in the different funeral services which are held across the various denominations.

In some Christian Churches, if someone is very sick and death seems near, a priest prepares them by saying special prayers.

## The sacrament of the sick

Roman Catholics have a sacrament called the sacrament of the sick. This sacrament is to bring comfort to the sick person. It assures them that God has forgiven them for their sins. They are strengthened to face the last few hours of their life. In this sacrament the priest rubs consecrated oil in the shape of a cross on the person's body. This is accompanied by prayers and the laying on of the priest's hands. The 'laying on of hands' is an old Christian tradition going back to Jesus and the disciples in the Gospels.

## The funeral service

In the Christian Church, the choice of whether a person is cremated or buried is left to the relatives. A similar service is used for both. Often a service is held in a church before the body is taken to the crematorium. In almost all funeral services, the comforting words of Psalm 23 are read out to assure everyone that God walks with the dead person through the 'valley of the shadow of death'.

Before the body is cremated or buried, words similar to these are said:

> We entrust our brother/sister to God's merciful keeping and we now commit his/her body to the ground. Earth to earth, ashes to ashes, dust to dust; in sure and certain hope of the resurrection to eternal life through our Lord Jesus Christ, who died, was buried and rose again for us. To Him be the glory for ever and ever. Amen.

If the body is being buried, a handful of earth is thrown on to the coffin as it is lowered into the grave. This is a symbol of the belief expressed in the prayer that at the end of life we return to the element from which we began life – earth.

The funeral service is intended to offer comfort for those who remain. The prayers, the Bible readings and the hymns thank God for the life of the person who has died. They also assure friends and relatives of the strong Christian hope that death is not the end. Death marks the beginning of eternal life. In the Roman Catholic Church, the service is a Requiem Mass in which a special celebration of Holy Communion takes place.

**B** The Christian funeral service is devised to bring comfort to those who remain

# At the moment of burial

As the coffin is lowered into the ground, the priest says:

*Man born of a woman has but a short time to live. Like a flower he blossoms and then withers; like a shadow he flees and never stays. In the midst of life we are in death; to whom can we turn for help but to you, O Lord, who are justly angered by our sins. Lord God, holy and mighty, holy and immortal, holy and most merciful Saviour, deliver us from the bitter pains of eternal death. You know the secrets of our hearts; in your mercy hear our prayer, forgive us our sins, and at the last hour let us not fall away from you.*

## Find the answers

- What is the sacrament of the sick?

- Which psalm is included in most funeral services?

- What is the name for the funeral service in the Roman Catholic Church?

## Learning about, learning from

1  a. Why does the priest say 'earth to earth, ashes to ashes, dust to dust' before a body is buried or cremated?
   b. What does this say about the Christian attitude to death?
   c. Describe what happens at a Christian funeral service.
2  What do you think Christians might:
   a. do to help people who are dying?
   b. do to help those who have a loved one who is dying?

## Extra activity

Read the quotation from the moment of burial in the box.
a. Why is a person's life likened to a flower that blossoms and dies or a shadow that flees?
b. What do you think is meant by the words 'in the midst of life we are in death'?

# Christianity and life after death

Christians hold very firmly to the belief that death is not the end but the beginning. This is based on their belief that, three days after he was crucified, Jesus was brought back to life by God. In the same way they, too, expect to be brought back to life at the end of time. This will happen when Christ returns to the earth to judge everyone. Only then will Christians be able to enter fully into the eternal life that God has promised them.

## Eternal life

Christians believe that even during their time on earth they have caught glimpses of

**A** Christians believe they can be confident of life after death because Jesus rose from the dead

eternal life. This is the life that Jesus came to bring them. At the same time, they look forward to the Second Coming when Jesus will return to the earth. However, when that happens he will not come as he did 2000 years ago – as a helpless baby. He will return as the judge to whom everyone will have to account for the lives they have lived.

One of the earliest statements of Christian belief, the Nicene Creed, was drawn up early in the fourth century CE. It says:

> He [Christ] will come in glory to judge the living and the dead... We look for the resurrection of the dead and the life of the world to come.

## The Day of Judgement

In the Bible there are many references to the Day of Judgement. Here are three of them:

- By Jesus: 'At that time they will see the Son of Man coming in a cloud with power and great glory.'
- By **Paul**: 'For the Lord himself will come down from heaven, with a loud command, with the voice of the archangel and with the trumpet call of God and the dead in Christ will rise first. After that, we who are still alive and are left will be caught up together with them in the clouds to meet the Lord in the air.'
- By Paul: 'We shall not all die, but when the last trumpet sounds, we shall all be changed in an instant, as quickly as the blinking of an eye. For when the trumpet sounds, the dead will be raised, never to die again.'

In the past, Christianity has taught that people who have led a good life are sent to heaven, where God is, and those who have

**B** Christians believe they will be brought back to life on the Day of Judgement

led an evil life are sent to hell for ever. However, most Christians today do not believe that heaven and hell are actual places. Rather, they are states of mind in which God is present (heaven) or absent (hell). The Roman Catholic Church teaches that the people who have lived a blameless life go directly to heaven, but the vast majority of people spend time in **purgatory**. It is there that souls are purified and made ready for heaven.

### In the glossary

Paul                    Purgatory

## The love of God

In one of his letters, Paul wrote:
*I am convinced that neither death nor life, nor angels nor demons, neither the present nor the future, neither height nor depth, nor anything else in the whole of creation, will be able to separate us from the love of God that is in Christ Jesus our Lord.*

 **Find the answers**

- On which event do Christians base their belief that death is not the end?

- When do Christians believe that eternal life begins?

- What do Christians expect to happen at the end of time?

 **Learning about, learning from**

**1 a.** What do Christians mean by the resurrection of Jesus?
  **b.** What comfort might this belief give someone who has just lost a loved one?

**2** Imagine you want to write a letter to a friend who has just lost someone close. What would you say to them? How would you try to comfort them?

**3** The descriptions on gravestones are called epitaphs. Write an epitaph that you would like to have placed on your own gravestone.

 **Extra activity**

Why are the ideas of resurrection and new life important to Christians?

# Jewish funerals

In Judaism, beliefs about life after death are not as clear as they are in other religions. Jews have always stressed the importance of living by God's laws in this life rather than trying to work out what happens in the next. They look forward to the time when the **Messiah**, God's messenger, will come to free them from their enemies. When this happens, a new time of hope will begin on earth for all people, not just Jews.

## Preparing for death

If a religious Jewish person becomes seriously ill and fears that death is close, they say a special prayer, which is in three parts:

**A** The gravestone is not erected on a Jewish grave until months after the person has died

- Confirming their belief in the one God who cares for them.
- Pleading for help from God to recover from the illness.
- Confessing their sins and showing a willingness to make good everything they may have done wrong.

## The funeral service

In the Jewish tradition, burial takes place as soon as possible after death. Cremation is not allowed because it involves the destruction of something – the human body – that God has created. If destroyed, the body could not be resurrected on the Day of Judgement. The body must be treated with great respect in death as in life. It is not left unattended from the moment of death through to its burial.

The body is wrapped in a simple linen cloth. This custom was introduced in the first century CE so that funerals could not be used as an opportunity for a family to show its wealth – linen was available to rich and poor alike. The Jewish community does not use professional undertakers. Every synagogue has a group of men and women who consider it an honour to prepare the body for burial. It is an act of loving kindness with no reward.

The funeral service itself is very brief. At the graveside the mourners recite a short prayer. They then use a spade to scatter some earth on top of the coffin, which has been lowered into the grave. The service ends with the words:

> The Lord has given and the Lord has taken away; blessed be the name of the Lord.

It is the custom to say the following words to the relatives of the person who has died:

> May God console you together with all the mourners of Zion and Jerusalem.

## Mourning

In Judaism, there are set periods of mourning to help relatives to come to terms with their loss. After the funeral, shiva begins. This is a week of deep mourning when relatives stay at home and say prayers three times a day. Friends take care of everyday jobs like cooking and cleaning. People in shiva are encouraged to talk about their bereavement so that they can begin to come to terms with it. This is followed by 30 days of lesser mourning, during which time the mourners begin to return to normal life. When a parent or partner has died, mourning continues for a full year after burial.

**B** In some synagogues a stained-glass window is made to commemorate a person's life

**In the glossary**
Messiah

 **Find the answers**
- What does a Jew pray for as death approaches?
- Why are Jews buried in a linen cloth?
- What is shiva?

**Learning about, learning from**

1 When someone has died, mourners often talk about them and how they remember them. Why do they do this? How do you think talking might help those who mourn?

2 **a.** Jews wrap the body in a simple linen cloth to show that all people, after death, are equal. Why is this important?
**b.** How could a funeral be turned into an opportunity for people to show off their wealth?

3 Why are the stages of mourning arranged as they are in Judaism? How might this help people come to terms with their grief?

4 A headstone cannot be erected in a Jewish cemetery until just before the first anniversary of a person's death. Why do you think this is?

 **Extra activity**

In Jewish writings, preparing a body for its burial is called 'a true kindness'. Why is it called this?

# Judaism and life after death

In Judaism, the emphasis is upon this life and not the next. However, most Jews believe that the soul comes from God and is immortal, so it cannot die when the body does. They also believe that the dead will be brought back to life on the Day of Judgement. As Moses Maimonides, a thirteenth-century rabbi, said:

> I believe with perfect faith that there will be a resurrection of the dead at a time when it shall please the Creator.

## The afterlife

The Jewish scriptures give some ideas about life after death, but they rarely go into any detail. Sheol appears to be the shadowy underworld home where the ghosts of the dead gather while waiting for their final resurrection. It is here that they are purified of their sins. It is only when they are purified that they can enter into the presence of God.

In this passage from the Jewish scriptures, the prophet Isaiah is looking forward to the doom that will swallow up the king of Babylon:

> The grave below is all astir to meet you at your coming; it rouses the spirits of the departed to greet you – all those who were leaders in the world; it makes them rise from their thrones – all those who were kings over the nations. They will respond, they will say to you, 'You have become weak, as we are; you have become like us. All your pomp has been brought down to the grave, along with the noise of your harps; maggots are spread out beneath you and worms cover you.

## Heaven and hell

The Jewish scriptures also hint at the idea of heaven and hell. Certainly many Jews believe that there will be reward and punishment after death, depending on the way people have lived in this life:

- If the person is good, and has proved it by the way he or she has lived in this life, heaven awaits.
- If the person is wicked, and has lived a life full of wrongdoing, hell is their destination.

Judaism does not teach that punishment is eternal. Many Jews believe that heaven can be reached through repentance, prayer and charity, but it is not clear whether heaven exists as an actual place or not. The traditional story told in the box suggests that heaven is a state of mind rather than a place to which people go after death. Many Jews who suffered so terribly at the hands of the Nazis in the Second World War believed they had experienced hell on earth.

**A** Jews believe that the dead will be brought back to life on the Day of Judgement

אֵין זֶה כִּי אִם בֵּית אֱלֹהִים
וְזֶה שַׁעַר הַשָּׁמָיִם

**B** Jews believe that the good will eventually reach heaven

## Heaven is here

An old Jewish story tells of a visitor to paradise who was amazed to find it filled up with old men taken up with studying the Torah.
Astonished, he turned to his heavenly guide, who told him:
*You are mistaken if you think these men are in heaven. Heaven is in these men.*

 **Find the answers**

- What do Jews call the shadowy underworld?

- When does Judaism say that the dead will be brought back to life?

- How do many Jews believe heaven can be reached?

 **Learning about, learning from**

**1** In these sentences the heads and tails have been mixed up. Unscramble them and write down the correct versions in your exercise book or file.

| | |
|---|---|
| In the Jewish faith the emphasis is upon | the home of the dead. |
| Sheol is | can be experienced on earth. |
| The soul comes from God | will take place at a time which is pleasing to God. |
| Many Jews believe that heaven and hell | living the present life. |
| According to Moses Maimonides, the resurrection of all people | and so cannot be destroyed. |

**2** There is no teaching in the Torah about life after death. Does this suggest that Jews should not be concerned with what happens after death? If so, do you think this is a sensible attitude to take?

 **Extra activity**

A Jewish cemetery is called the House of Life. Explain why you think this is.

# Muslim funerals

Muslims believe that the time will come when all life on earth will end and people will have their deeds judged by Allah. On their deathbed, Muslims try to make peace with God. Just as they heard the Shahadah from their father soon after they were born, so they hope this statement of faith will be the last thing they say before they die:

> There is no God but Allah and Muhammad is the Messenger of Allah.

If the believer is too weak to speak these final words, someone else can say them on their behalf.

## The funeral service

As soon as a person has died, their hands are laid across the chest as if they were worshipping Allah. The body is then washed by someone of the same sex. It is wrapped in three simple sheets of cloth to show that everyone is equal in death. The body is then placed on a wooden frame or in a coffin and carried to the place of prayer. This may be a mosque or another clean place. Here the body is laid out for a short service, with the head turned towards the holy city of **Makkah**.

**A** Muslims hope that the Shahadah will be the last words to cross their lips before they die

Muslims always bury rather than cremate their dead. After prayers have been said, it is lowered into the grave, with the head turned slightly to face the **Ka'bah**, the holy shrine in Makkah. As this happens these words are repeated several times:

> With the name of God and on the religion of the Messenger of God.

It is the tradition that the body should be in direct contact with the earth when it is buried. In Britain, however, the law says that a body must be buried in a coffin. A special case is made for Muslims, who are allowed to bury their dead with the coffin turned upside-down over the body.

In Islam it is forbidden to spend a lot of money on a funeral or on the graves of those who have died. Instead, Muslims believe the money is better spent on the poor and needy, with the prayer that the blessings which come from giving to others should go to the one who has died.

Muslims who live in Britain sometimes send the body to a Muslim country so that it can be buried alongside other Muslims. As the size of the Muslim community in Britain grows, however, this happens less often. There are now Muslim cemeteries in many of the large towns and cities in the United Kingdom.

## Mourning

Officially, seven days are set aside in a Muslim family to mourn a lost one. Some Muslim communities, however, also have 40 days of readings from the Qur'an in a person's memory. During the seven days of mourning, the family stays at home and receives visitors, who pray that Allah will show mercy on the deceased. It is the responsibility of the family, especially the children, to make sure that the memory of the loved one is always kept alive.

**B** Muslims are buried facing the holy city of Makkah

# Visited by two angels

Muslims believe the dead person is visited by two angels, who put certain questions to him or her. To help them with the answers, these words are said over the grave after burial:

*O male – or female – servant of God, remember the covenant made while leaving the world, that is, the statement that there is no God but God Himself, and that Muhammad is the Messenger of God, and the belief that paradise is a truth, that the Doomsday shall come, there being no doubt about it; that God will bring back to life those who are in the graves, that thou hast accepted God as they Lord, Islam as thy religion, Muhammad as thy prophet, the Qur'an as thy guide, the Ka'bah as thy direction to turn to for the service of worship and that all believers are thy brethren. May God keep thee firm in this trial.*

**In the glossary**

Ka'bah          Makkah

 **Find the answers**

- What words does a Muslim hope will be the last on his lips before he dies?
- How do Muslims show that, in death, everyone is equal?
- How is the importance of Makkah recognised in death?

 **Learning about, learning from**

1 Write a sentence about each of the following.
   **a.** The importance of the Shahadah at the end of life.
   **b.** The preparation of the body for burial.
   **c.** The placing of the body in the grave.
   **d.** Spending money on the funeral.

2 **a.** In the quotation in the box about the visit of two angles, the Muslim believer is told of eleven things they can have complete confidence in. Make a list of them.
   **b.** What is the final hope and prayer for the dead person?

 **Extra activity**

Why do you think that, if possible, a Muslim is buried in the same clothes that he or she wore whilst going on the Hajj?

# Islam and life after death

Muslims are not afraid of death. They believe it is simply the state of the body as the soul moves from one form of life to the next. Because of this, they are more concerned with life after death, **akhirah**, than many of the other religions.

## The Day of Judgement

The Qur'an warns people that a frightening Day of Judgement is coming, when every man and woman will have to appear before Allah to account for the way they have lived. The Qur'an teaches that on that day:

- The skies will be split from top to bottom.
- The stars will scatter.
- The oceans will roll together.
- The graves will be hurled about.

When this happens, each soul will know what it has done and what it has failed to do. Allah, the judge of mankind, will divide the human race into two groups as described in the Qur'an:

> Those on the right hand (blessed be those on the right)... they shall recline on jewelled couches face to face, and there shall wait on them immortal youths with bowls and ewers [jugs] and a cup of purest wine... a gushing fountain shall be there and raised soft couches with goblets placed before them; silken cushions richly ranged in order and carpets richly spread... those on the left (damned be those on the left)... they shall dwell amidst scorching winds and boiling water... their only food shall be bitter thorns, which shall neither sustain them nor satisfy their hunger.

## Paradise and hell

The Qur'an contains detailed descriptions of paradise and hell. However, most Muslims do not think of them as real places but as symbols. The Qur'an states clearly that the afterlife is beyond all human understanding. According to the holy book, when they die everyone must cross a bridge over the bottomless pit of hell. Those who have lived a good life cross straight over and enter paradise. As picture A shows, they immediately begin to enjoy all the good things that Allah has prepared for them. Heaven is a place of unending delight.

The wicked, however, fall from the bridge into the gaping jaws of hell. Hell and its torments are eternal – they last for ever. It is the place which Allah has prepared for all those who have lived evil lives and have refused to accept that Muhammad is the prophet of Allah. It is a place of everlasting fear and punishment.

**A** The Muslim heaven is a place of everlasting pleasure

**B** Muslims believe that hell is a place of everlasting torment for the wicked

# God, the Merciful

Although the Qur'an describes God as a severe figure of judgement, He is also called the Merciful. In a chapter called 'The Resurrection', the Qur'an says:
*On that day there shall be joyous faces, looking towards their Lord. On that day there shall be mournful faces dreading some great affliction.*

---

**In the glossary**

Akhirah

---

 **Find the answers**

- What is akhirah?

- Into which two groups will mankind be divided on the Day of Judgement?

- What do people cross before they enter heaven or hell?

 **Learning about, learning from**

**1** Fit together the following phrases to make a sensible paragraph. The first phrase is in place for you.

| | |
|---|---|
| Muslims believe that | God will judge all people. |
| On that day all people | on the Day of Judgement |
| Those on the left | will be divided into two groups. |
| They are most blessed of all. | will be sent to hell. |
| Those on the right hand | will be sent to paradise. |

**2** Write a paragraph about each of the following.
   **a.** How Muslims understand heaven.
   **b.** How Muslims understand hell.

**3 a.** What do you think happens after death?
   **b.** Do your views on life after death bear any similarity to those held by Muslims?

 **Extra activity**

Can you identify two similarities and two differences between the Christian, Jewish and Muslim ideas about life after death?

# Hindu funerals

Hindus believe that one lifetime is nowhere near long enough to decide a person's eternal destiny. When someone dies, the soul lives on in a new body. This is called reincarnation. Although sadness and mourning are natural for the relatives of the deceased, they can, by performing the correct ceremonies, make sure that the soul makes a suitable entry into the next life.

## The funeral service

A person's funeral is their sixteenth, and last, samskara. The Hindu tradition is that the body should be burned within a few hours of death. Cremation by fire is usual because fire purifies the soul. It is only the souls of saintly people like priests, and those of newborn babies, which do not need purification. For these people, burial rather than cremation is normal.

The dearest wish of every Hindu is that they should die close enough to the River Ganges to have their ashes scattered on its waters. If this happens, the soul does not need to enter into another body but can pass directly into paradise. Sometimes the ashes of Hindus who die in another country are brought to India to be scattered on the Ganges. If this cannot happen, they are scattered on the waters of any stream, river or sea. Hindus believe that all the waters of the earth come together in the oceans.

It is the solemn responsibility of the eldest son in a Hindu family to light the funeral pyre of a parent. It is important that the funeral ceremonies are carried out carefully or the soul of the dead person may return and become a ghost. This is why all Hindu parents hope for at least one son because he alone can carry out the funeral ceremony properly.

As the fire reaches the body on the pyre, the son pours ghee (clarified butter) on to the flames. The priest begins to chant mantras as the flames burn up the body. Three days later, the son returns to gather up the ashes. Then, in the days following the cremation, important ceremonies are carried out at home by members of the dead person's family. These rites are to help the soul find a new body in which to enter the next life.

The final rites are carried out on the tenth, eleventh and twelfth days after death. Milk and rice offerings are made for the dead person. A separate ceremony, performed on the eleventh day, marks the time when Hindus believe that the soul is free to enter the next life. Mourning can last for as long as 13 days and during this time the close family has no contact with the outside world.

A After death the body of a Hindu is burned quickly, often on the banks of the River Ganges

**B** Pilgrims come to the River Ganges to bathe in the waters where they hope their ashes will one day be scattered

# Taking the last journey

Travellers are a common sight in India. In this extract from one of the Hindu holy books, which is often used at funerals, the dead person is compared to a traveller:

*Worn-out garments are shed by the body, worn-out bodies are shed by the traveller. Within the body new bodies are put on by the dweller, like garments.*

 **Learning about, learning from**

1  **a.** What is reincarnation?
   **b.** How do you think a belief in reincarnation might affect the way someone lives today?

2  The Bhagavad Gita, a Hindu holy book, says this about dying: 'As a man leaves his old clothes and puts on new ones, so the soul leaves the body and moves to a new one.'
   **a.** Why is death compared with taking off one set of clothes and putting on another?
   **b.** Does it help to think of death in this way?

3  Hindus scatter the ashes of a loved one on to water. Explain one reason why they do this.

 **Extra activity**

In the quotation in the box, a dead person is likened to a traveller. What do you think this statement is intended to teach?

**Find the answers**

- What does a Hindu believe happens to the body at death?

- Who carries out the funeral rites?

- How do members of a Hindu family help the soul to find another home?

# Hinduism and life after death

To Hindus, what is immortal (undying) in every human being is the Brahman or Supreme Spirit. Everything comes in the first place from God and returns in the end to Him. The soul, reborn many times, is searching for this union with Brahman. The box on the next page contains a popular prayer from one of the Hindu holy books, the Upanishads, which expresses this thought.

## Union with Brahman

There are three ways in Hinduism that a human being can try to reach union with Brahman. Each way is known as a **yoga**:

- The way of unselfish service. By helping others and putting them first, the human soul hopes to reach God eventually. Although there are other ways by which God can be reached, it is the unselfish people who are most likely to find him.
- The way of devotion. Many Hindus believe their only realistic hope of achieving union with God lies in a faithful worship of their own particular family god. It is the mother's responsibility to make sure that worship is arranged within the family and that the proper offerings of fruit, flowers and incense are presented at the home shrine.
- The way of knowledge. Some Hindu men believe that through a study of the holy books and by leading a very holy life that they can achieve union with God. When they are no longer needed in family life, they may take themselves off to live the life of a **sadhu**, a travelling holy man. However, few Hindus achieve their goal because it is an almost impossible task to master all the Hindu holy books.

Whichever way a Hindu chooses to reach the final union with Brahman, they all agree that one life is far too short a time for the task. It is unthinkable that God should choose to decide the destiny of a human soul on the basis of one lifetime. Thousands of rebirths are needed before any individual soul can reach its goal.

## Karma

Karma is a belief which is strongly held by Hindus. It is at the heart of their belief in reincarnation. It teaches that the actions a person carries out in this life will determine their rewards or punishments in the next life. Luck plays no part in this process. Every person makes their own future by choosing the way they live now. Good actions mean good karma and bad actions result in bad karma. If a person returns at a lower level of life, it is their fault and no one else's. The law of karma cannot be altered.

A Many Hindus believe that their only hope of reaching union with God is the faithful worship of their family god

B Some Hindus believe that they can reach union with Brahman through studying the holy books and living a holy life

# Immortality

These words are taken from one of the most important Hindu holy books, the Upanishads:

*From the unreal lead me to the real,*
*From darkness lead me to light,*
*From death lead me to immortality.*

## In the glossary

Sadhu                    Yoga

 **Find the answers**

- What do Hindus believe the human soul is searching for?

- How many ways are there for humans to achieve union with Brahman?

- What is a yoga?

 **Learning about, learning from**

1  Write two sentences about each of the following yogas.
   **a.** The way of unselfish service.
   **b.** The way of devotion.
   **c.** The way of knowledge.
   Give an example for each of these ways in which a Hindu might hope to reach union with Brahman.

2  What is karma? Explain what it means in no more than three sentences.

 **Extra activity**

Do you think people should be frightened of the consequences when they do wrong things?

# Sikh funerals

**A** To Sikhs, death is no more than a brief sleep

According to Sikh belief, everyone has a body and a soul. At death the body dies but the soul cannot be destroyed. It is indestructible. The soul continues to be reborn until it is finally reunited with God. As the Guru Granth Sahib says:

> The drop of water [the soul] is in the ocean [God] and the quality of the ocean is in the water.

## As death approaches

As the time of death draws close, a Sikh is encouraged to repeat over and over again the phrase 'Waheguru, Waheguru', which means 'Wonderful Lord, Wonderful Lord'. At the same time, someone reads out extracts from the Guru Granth Sahib to comfort the dying person. After death, the body is washed. If the deceased belonged to the Khalsa, they are dressed in the symbols of the Five Ks. Hymns are also read aloud.

## The funeral service

Some families take the body of a loved one to the gurdwara while others choose to keep the coffin at home. They look at the body for the last time and say their farewells. The body is then carried by members of the Sikh community to the place set aside for cremation. The funeral pyre is lit by a close relative. At the same time, the words of the sohilla, the evening hymn, are chanted:

> Strive to seek that for which thou hast come into the world and through the grace of the Guru, God will dwell in thy heart.

For Sikhs, death is no more than a brief sleep and so the Guru Granth Sahib does not contain any prayers for the dead.

## After the funeral

In Britain, cremations must take place in a crematorium. By tradition once a body has been burned the ashes must be scattered on the waters of a flowing river. Sikhs in Britain may do this on the tidal waters of a river or take them out on to the open sea. Sometimes the ashes are sent to relatives in India, who scatter them in the traditional way.

After the cremation, relatives begin a reading of the whole Guru Granth Sahib, called an **Akhand Path**. This can take 48 hours, but in most cases it lasts for ten days. This takes place in the house of the deceased to bring comfort to the relatives. In total, mourning in a Sikh family lasts for ten days. Although Sikhs show their grief for the loss of a loved one, they should not show excessive sadness. They are also not allowed to build any memorials to the dead. Sikhs believe that the words and deeds of the dead live on in the memories of those who remain. These are their true monuments (see the box on the next page).

If the dead person was the head of the family, the new head of the family may be given turbans by his friends and relatives to symbolise his new position of authority.

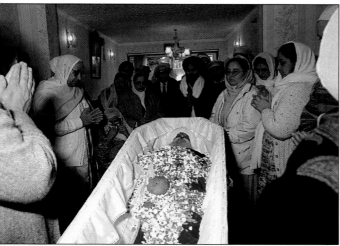

**B** The coffin is left open until the last possible moment so that everyone can say their farewells

## The living and the dead

The Guru Granth Sahib says:
*The dead keep their link with the living through their virtuous deeds.*

### In the glossary
Akhand Path

## Find the answers

- What does a Sikh try to say as death draws near?

- What happens to the ashes of a Sikh?

- What happens in a Sikh family directly after the cremation has taken place?

## Learning about, learning from

1  a. What do Sikhs believe happens to the soul after death?
   b. Why did Guru Nanak teach that reincarnation helps people to make sense of life?

2  a. Why are Sikh relatives deeply involved in the preparation of a body for a funeral?
   b. Do you think such involvement might help someone to come to terms with their loss?

3  If there is a religious service in the gurdwara or at the home of the deceased, or if there is an Akhand Path, karah parshad is given out.
   a. Remembering what you have learnt about Sikh worship, can you think of two other occasions when karah parshad is distributed?
   b. What does this tell you about the importance of these occasions?

## Extra activity

a. Why is crying for someone who has died discouraged by Sikhs?
b. Which beliefs prevent Sikhs from seeing death as the end?

# Sikhism and life after death

**A** Sikhs believe in reincarnation, with the soul passing through many rebirths before it returns to God

The founder of Sikhism, Guru Nanak, accepted that there are many ways of finding God. He did not share the view of many other religions, which hold that each person spends one life on earth followed by eternity in either heaven or hell. In the Japji Sahib, a prayer found at the beginning of the Guru Granth Sahib, Guru Nanak said:

> By his writ some have pleasures, others pain,
> By His Grace some are saved,
> Others doomed to die, relive and die again;
> His will encompasseth all, there is none beside,
> O Nanak, he who knows, hath no ego and no pride.

## Reincarnation

Sikhs believe that every human being is made up of soul and body. The body is not particularly important as it is only the vehicle that carries the soul on its journey to God. The soul belongs to the spiritual universe of God. Sikhs believe that when the body dies the soul is born again in another form. This happens time and time again until eventually it is reunited with God, who alone is the Truth. This is called reincarnation, a belief that Sikhs share with Hindus and Buddhists.

## Reaching God

Sikhism teaches its followers that they are not bad by nature. At the beginning of time God created everyone good, but they were overcome by selfishness. The soul, the spiritual part of everyone, is a very small part of the Supreme Being, God. Through many reincarnations the soul will return at last to God.

The supreme goal of every religious Sikh is when life finally comes to an end and the soul meets God. Guru Nanak taught that, with God's grace and goodness, everyone can reach the Truth – the powerful and the powerless, the rich and the poor, the beggars and the rulers, both male and female. Good behaviour in the present life, such as caring for the poor and needy, leads to a higher form of life in the next. Selfish behaviour in the present life, however, leads to a lower form of life in the next.

Guru Arjan encouraged all Sikhs to look forward to the time when they would be reunited with God:

> Since you have now acquired this human frame,
> This is your opportunity to become one with God;
> All other labours are of no use,
> Seek the company of the holy and glorify God's name.

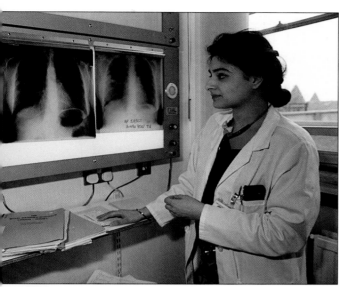

 Sikhs believe that caring for the needy in this life leads to rebirth in a higher form in the next

## Life and death

The Guru Granth Sahib says:
*By God's decree all souls come into being,*
*They engage in activity as decreed by him,*
*By his decree they are subject to death,*
*And according to this decree*
*They are merged in Truth.*

### Find the answers

- What is the Sikh belief about life after death called?
- How do Sikhs believe that the cycle of birth, life, death and rebirth is finalled ended?
- What is the final goal of every Sikh?

 **Learning about, learning from**

1 Read the quotes by Guru Nanak and Guru Arjan in the text.
   a. Who decides whether, in this life, some people have pleasure while others have pain?
   b. Which line makes clear the Sikh belief in reincarnation?
   c. Who do you think Guru Nanak is referring to when he speaks of the one who 'hath no ego and no pride'?
   d. What should a person's only concern in this life be?

2 There are two main beliefs about life after death in the world's major six religions.
   a. What are these beliefs?
   b. Make a table to show which religions teach which belief.
   c. What are the main differences between these two approaches to life after death?
   d. Which of the two viewpoints are you most inclined to accept? Explain your answer.

### Extra activity

Read the quotation from the Guru Granth Sahib in the box.
a. Four things are decreed by God for all humankind. What are they?
b. What do you think the final phrase 'and according to this decree they are merged in Truth' means?

# Buddhist funerals

Throughout their lives, Buddhists remind themselves that everyone's life comes to an end at some time, even their own. While close relatives and friends are naturally sad at the death of a loved one, they are encouraged to remain cheerful in the face of death. One of the four sights that made Siddhartha Gotama set off in search for enlightenment was seeing a funeral procession. This shows how important death is to the Buddhist understanding of life.

## The funeral service

When a Buddhist dies, the family look after the body and wash it carefully. In some communities it is then laid in a wooden coffin, adorned with flowers and carried to the shrine room in the temple. Offerings are placed in front of the statues of the Buddha. Blessings are repeated, such as:

> Reverencing the Buddha we offer flowers,
> Flowers that today are fresh and sweetly blooming,
> Flowers that tomorrow are faded and fallen,
> Our bodies too like flowers will pass away.

As the monks make their way to the funeral, they chat happily with the people they pass. They carry with them pieces of paper, which are inserted into prayer sticks. On these are written texts from the holy books, which speak of how all life must end. The monks are deeply involved in the funeral, talking to people and distributing the pieces of paper to the mourners. This gains merit for the priests and also helps the mourners to understand the meaning of death. They also express the hope that everyone, in the end, will reach nirvana. By giving gifts to members of the sangha (the community of monks), the mourners hope to make some progress towards their final goal. This wish is often included in any notice of the death that has been placed in a newspaper or elsewhere.

It is important that relatives and friends remember the deceased in the weeks and months after the cremation. Thoughts that carry their best wishes are believed to help them achieve a good rebirth. Children are expected to hold a memorial service for a dead parent 100 days after the death. It is expected that the feelings of grief will have subsided by this time and children will be able to think of their dead parent with gratitude and thanksgiving.

## Relics

When the person who has died is a buddha (an enlightened one), a saint or a great teacher, relics are collected after the cremation. These may be placed in a **stupa** or in an image of the Buddha. Whenever a Buddhist sees a stupa in the countryside or an image of the Buddha in the temple, it is a reminder of the teaching of the Buddha. This is the reason why stupas and images are very highly honoured.

**A** One of the four sights of Siddhartha Gotama was that of a funeral procession

**B** These prayers for mourners are attached to a tree outside a monastry

# Gathering life's flowers

The Buddha said the following about death:

*Death carries off a man who is gathering life's flowers whose mind is distracted, even as a flood carries off a sleeping village. All created things are impermanent, when one by wisdom realises this, he heeds not this world of sorrow.*

## In the glossary
**Stupa**

 **Find the answers**

- What do monks carry with them as they travel to a funeral?
- What do monks hope to gain by attending a funeral?
- How do ordinary Buddhists hope to progress towards nirvana at a funeral?

**Learning about, learning from**

1 Design a poster to explain what happens during a Buddhist funeral and what Buddhists believe about life and death.

2 Read the quotation by the Buddha in the box. What did the Buddha mean when he spoke of death as being like the carrying off of a man who is gathering life's flowers?

3 **a.** Do you think it is possible to accept fully that in life death is inevitable? Is this something that young people, in particular, are inclined to forget?
**b.** If you accepted fully that the whole of your life was leading to death, would it make a difference to the way you lived?

 **Extra activity**

What does Buddhism teach about life that enables a Buddhist to accept death calmly?

# Nirvana

Nirvana is the goal of every Buddhist, but it is not easy to understand. The word itself gives us a clue. It means the blowing out of the flames of a fire so that they no longer exist. Samsara is the repeated cycle of birth, life, death and rebirth. This has been likened to being trapped in a burning building without realising it. Three fires are burning inside all of us – the fires of greed, hatred and delusion (not holding the right views about life). Buddhism is the 'fire alarm' that warns us of these fires. Only when they are all extinguished can nirvana be reached.

**A** The Wheel of Life shows that Buddhists are certain that, after many rebirths, the fires of hatred, greed and delusion will be put out

## Entering nirvana

Buddhists are certain that, after many rebirths, the fires of hatred, greed and delusion will be put out. Then the soul will enter nirvana. One of the ways that brings nirvana closer is for someone to help someone else along the pathway. This wins them merit and so is an important stage on the journey.

However, what exactly is the state towards which all Buddhists are moving? They believe nirvana cannot be described. It is completely beyond human language. When the Buddha tried to describe what nirvana was like to some of his followers, he was forced to say what it was *not* rather than what it *was*:

> Monks, there is that sphere wherein is neither earth nor water, fire nor air; it is not the infinity of space, nor the infinity of perception; it is not nothingness, nor is it either idea or non-idea; it is neither this world nor the next, nor is it both; it is neither the sun nor the moon. Monks, I say it neither comes nor goes; it neither abides nor passes away; it is not caused, established, begun, supported; it is the end of suffering.

In other words, nirvana is not like anything else. There is nothing with which it can be compared. It cannot be referred to anything else that people can understand. Nirvana is out on its own, beyond description and understanding. It is a state to be enjoyed and experienced, not to be described. When there is no longer any wax to be burned, the candle simply stops burning and expires. Similarly, nirvana is that higher state of consciousness in which all greed, hatred and delusion are burned out.

However, there is one thing that can be said about nirvana. The whole of Buddhism is concerned with explaining and presenting an answer to suffering. In nirvana there is no suffering. One of the Buddhist holy books says:

Medicine puts an end to bodily ills. Precisely so, nirvana puts a final end to all sufferings.

**B** Bodhissatvas are buddhas who choose to remain behind on earth to teach people how to reach nirvana

## Nirvana

One of the most well-known Buddhist books is based on the questions of a Greek king to a Buddhist monk. In one of his answers, the monk, Nagasena, said the following about nirvana:
*Great king, just as although the great ocean exists, it is impossible to measure the water or count the living beings that make their abode there, precisely so, great king, although nirvana really exists, it is impossible to make clear the form or figure or age or dimensions of nirvana.*

 **Find the answers**

- What is nirvana?
- What is samsara?
- Which three fires burn inside every human being?

 **Learning about, learning from**

1 In Japan, Buddhists put food as well as flowers on the graves of loved ones. Find out the significance of placing food on graves.

2 Buddhists describe nirvana as a state of bliss, totally free from all desire and suffering. They see nirvana as the perfect place. If you could create the perfect place for yourself, what would it be like? Remember that it must be the kind of place where you would wish to spend eternity.

3 Buddhists believe that there are three fires burning inside each of us.
   a. Give an example from everyday life of each of these fires.
   b. What do you think Buddhism means when it suggests that the endless cycle of samsara is like being trapped in a burning house without realising the seriousness of the plight?

 **Extra activity**

Read the extract about nirvana in the box. In your own words, explain the point the monk Nagasena was making.

# Glossary

**A**

**Abraham** The person considered by Jews to be the father of the Jewish nation; Muslims believe him to be one of the prophets.

**Absolution** The pronouncement by a priest that a person's sins have been forgiven; most likely to happen in the Roman Catholic and some Anglican churches.

**Adhan** The Muslim call to prayer, given from the minaret of the mosque.

**Akhand Path** The unbroken reading of the Guru Granth Sahib in the gurdwara; usually carried out on some special occasion.

**Akhirah** The Muslim belief in life after death.

**Allah** The name in Islam for God in the Arabic language.

**Altar** The raised platform at the eastern end of most churches, from where worship is conducted.

**Amrit** Holy water made from sugar and water; used by Sikhs in their initiation ceremonies such as the naming of a child or becoming a member of the faith.

**Amrit Sanskar** The Sikh ceremony at which members are initiated into the faith.

**Anand karaj** The Sikh wedding ceremony; the 'ceremony of bliss'.

**Anglican Church** Churches worldwide which follow the teachings of the Church of England and which accept the leadership of the Archbishop of Canterbury.

**Aqiqah** The initiation ceremony carried out on young children in Islam.

**Ardas** The most important Sikh prayer; draws every act of worship in the gurdwara to a close.

**Aum** The Hindu sacred syllable; believed to contain the sound of all reality.

**B**

**Baisakhi** An important Sikh festival which celebrates the formation of the Khalsa in 1699 CE.

**Baptism** The service of initiation for most Christian Churches; linked with the washing away of sins.

**Baptist Church** Nonconformist Church; believes in the baptism of adults not children.

**Bar mitzvah** 'Son of the commandment'; a Jewish boy's coming of age at 13 years old, marked by a ceremony and family celebration.

**Bat chayil** 'Daughter of worth'; the service held in Orthodox synagogues to celebrate a Jewish girl's coming of age at 12 years old.

**Bat mitzvah** 'Daughter of the commandment'; a Jewish girl's coming of age at 12 years old.

**Believer's baptism** The baptism of adults in the Baptist Church.

**Bhagavad Gita** A Hindu holy book.

**Bible** The Christian scriptures containing the Old and New Testaments; used by Christians in private and public worship.

**Bishop** A senior priest who carries the responsibility for all the churches in an area, ordains priests and performs confirmations.

**Brahma** The Hindu Creator God.

**Brahman** The Supreme God in Hinduism; the holy power which runs through the whole universe.

**Buddha** Siddhartha Gotama, who became the Enlightened One; gave the teaching upon which Buddhism is based.

**C**

**Celibacy** The requirement not to marry or have any sexual relationships.

**Chrismation** The name given to service in the Orthodox Church in which a baby is both baptised and confirmed.

**Christmas** The Christian festival which is celebrated on 25 December; commemorates the birth of Jesus.

**Church of England** The main Christian Church in Britain; also called the Anglican Church.

**Circumcision** An operation carried out on male babies in both Judaism and Islam at eight days old; involves the removal of the foreskin of the boy's penis.

**Citadel** Salvation Army place of worship.

**Confession** A sacrament of the Catholic Church; a meeting at which a priest hears a person's confession of sins and grants them God's forgiveness.

| | | |
|---|---|---|
| | **Confirmation** | A service in some Churches in which a person 'confirms' the promises that others made for them when they were baptised. |
| | **Creed** | A traditional statement of Christian belief. |
| **D** | **Divine Liturgy** | The name given to the service of Holy Communion in the Orthodox Church. |
| | **Du'a** | Personal prayers in Islam; prayers which are voluntary and not compulsory. |
| | **Dukkha** | The first of the Four Noble Truths in Buddhism, which says that suffering is in the nature of human existance. |
| **E** | **Easter** | The Christian festival at which believers remember and celebrate the death and resurrection of Jesus. |
| | **Exodus** | The journey out of Egyptian slavery taken by the Jews to the country of Canaan (Israel). |
| **F** | **Five Ks** | The five symbols given to all who become members of the Sikh Khalsa. |
| | **Font** | A stone or wooden receptacle inside many churches; holds the water that is used in infant baptism. |
| | **Four Noble Truths** | The beliefs on which the teaching of Buddhism are based; deal with the existence of suffering and the answer to it. |
| **G** | **Ganesha** | One of the most popular Hindu gods; has the head of an elephant. |
| | **Gospels** | Four books at the beginning of the New Testament in the Bible; each Gospel describes the life and teaching of Jesus. |
| | **Granthi** | An official in a gurdwara who reads the Guru Granth Sahib many times a day; officiates at Sikh services and ceremonies. |
| | **Gurdwara** | 'The doorway to the Guru'; the Sikh place of worship. |
| | **Guru** | Teacher; in Sikhism the title is used only for the ten human Gurus, for the Guru Granth Sahib and for God – the 'True Guru'. |
| | **Guru Granth Sahib** | The Sikh scriptures, which were put together by Guru Arjan and completed by Guru Gobind Singh. |
| | **Guru Nanak** | The first Guru; the founder of the Sikh faith (1469–1539 CE). |
| **H** | **Holocaust** | The murder of six million Jews by the Nazis during the Second World War. |
| | **Holy Communion** | The service held in most Christian Churches to commemorate the death of Jesus; also called the Mass, Divine Liturgy, Eucharist and Lord's Supper. |
| | **Holy Spirit** | The third person in the Christian Trinity with God the Father and God the Son. |
| **I** | **Iconostasis** | The screen, covered with icons, which separates the congregation from the altar in an Orthodox church. |
| | **Icons** | Special paintings of Jesus, the family of Jesus, the Virgin Mary or a saint; used as an aid to prayer in the Orthodox Church. |
| | **Imam** | The man who leads the prayers and preaches the Friday sermon in a mosque. |
| | **Infant baptism** | The practice of baptising babies; followed by most Churches including the Roman Catholic, Orthodox and Anglican Churches. |
| | **Israel** | Also called Palestine; the modern country of Israel was formed in 1948. |
| **K** | **Ka'bah** | The cube-shaped shrine which stands in Makkah; visited by millions of pilgrims during the Hajj. |
| | **Kachs** | One of the Five Ks; shorts worn as an undergarment. |
| | **Kangha** | One of the Five Ks; a comb. |
| | **Kara** | One of the Five Ks; a steel bracelet. |
| | **Karah parshad** | Food eaten at the end of services in a gurdwara. |
| | **Karma** | 'Action' or 'deed'; the Hindu belief that what a person does in this life leads to rewards or punishments in the next life. |
| | **Kesh** | One of the Five Ks; uncut hair. |

| | | |
|---|---|---|
| | Ketubah | The Jewish wedding contract. |
| | Khalsa | The Sikh religious brotherhood open to male and female believers; begun by the tenth Guru, Guru Gobind Singh, in 1699 CE. |
| | Kirpan | One of the Five Ks; a short sword. |
| **L** | Langar | 'Guru's kitchen'; the dining hall in a gurdwara and the food served there. |
| **M** | Mahayana Buddhism | One of the two main schools of Buddhism. |
| | Makkah | The birthplace of Muhammad in present-day Saudi Arabia. |
| | Mantra | A sacred formula or chant; used particularly in Hindu worship. |
| | Mass | The name given by Roman Catholics to the service of Holy Communion. |
| | Meeting houses | Places of worship for Quakers. |
| | Messiah | The figure expected by Jews to lead them out of captivity; Christians believe that Jesus was the promised Messiah. |
| | Methodist Church | The Nonconformist Church founded in the eighteenth century by John Wesley. |
| | Minister | A church leader in a Nonconformist Church. |
| | Monastery | The building where monks live. |
| | Monks | Men who devote themselves to a life of prayer and study; important in both Christianity and Buddhism. |
| | Mool Mantar | The statement of Sikh belief; the opening chapter of the Guru Granth Sahib. |
| | Moses | The man who led the Jews out of Egyptian slavery; received the Ten Commandments and the Jewish Law from God on Mount Sinai. |
| | Mosque | 'Place of prostration'; the Muslim place of worship. |
| | Muhammad | The last, and greatest, prophet in Islam; the one chosen by Allah to receive the revelations which are collected in the Qur'an. |
| | Murtis | Hindu images or statues of God. |
| **N** | Nam | The Sikh name for God. |
| | New Testament | The second part of the Christian Bible; it contains 27 books including the Gospels and the Epistles (letters) written by the early Christian leaders. |
| | Nirvana | The final state of perfect peace which all Buddhists strive for. |
| | Nonconformist Churches | Protestant Churches, such as the Baptist Church or Methodist Church, which separated from the Church of England in the seventeenth century. |
| **O** | Old Testament | The Jewish scriptures included as the first part of the Christian Bible; contains 39 books. |
| | Orthodox Church | Originally the Church of the Eastern region of the Roman Empire; separated from the Roman Catholic Church in 1054 CE. |
| **P** | Panj piares | 'The five beloved ones'; those who were first initiated into Khalsa and the name used for those who perform the rite today. |
| | Passover | The Jewish festival which commemorates the delivery of the Jews from slavery in Egypt. |
| | Paul | The leader of the early Christian Church; a missionary and writer of many books in the New Testament. |
| | Penance | The penalty imposed by a priest on someone who has confessed their sins. |
| | Peter | The main disciple of Jesus; became the first leader of the Christian Church after Jesus had left the earth. |
| | Pope | The head of the Roman Catholic Church; the Bishop of Rome. |
| | Priest | Someone ordained to the ministry in the Roman Catholic and Anglican Churches; given the authority to deliver the sacraments to the people. |
| | Prophets | Men or women who pass on God's message to the people. |
| | Protestant Church | Churches which do not belong to the Roman Catholic or Orthodox Churches. |
| | Purgatory | The place where Roman Catholics go after death and before entering heaven. |

| | | |
|---|---|---|
| **Q** | Quakers | The Christian Church formed in the seventeenth century by George Fox; known for its largely silent form of worship and also known as the Society of Friends. |
| | Qur'an | 'That which is read or recited'; the divine book revealed to the Prophet Muhammad by Allah. |
| **R** | Rabbis | Leaders of worship and teachers in a Jewish synagogue. |
| | Reincarnation | The belief held by Hindus and Buddhists that the soul is reborn many times before being released. |
| | Roman Catholic Church | The oldest Christian Church; owes its allegiance to the Pope in Rome. |
| **S** | Sabbath Day | The seventh day of the week; a Jewish day of rest which lasts from Friday night to Saturday night. |
| | Sacraments | Special Christian services in which God's blessing is given through a physical object such as bread, wine, oil or water. |
| | Sacred thread | The ceremony to mark the beginning of adulthood for many Hindu boys. |
| | Sadhu | A Hindu holy man. |
| | Salvation Army | The Protestant Church founded in the nineteenth century; known for its social work as well as its services. |
| | Samsara | The wheel of rebirth; the world. |
| | Samskaras | Ceremony associated with a stage in the lifecycle in Hinduism. |
| | Sangha | The Buddhist monastic order. |
| | Sermon | A part of the service in church when a passage from the Bible is explained. |
| | Shahadah | One of the Five Pillars of Islam; the statement of belief that Allah is the only God and Muhammad is Allah's messenger. |
| | Shema | A passage from the Jewish scriptures which underlines that God is one; used in most Jewish services. |
| | Shiva | One of the greatest Hindu gods. |
| | Stupa | Originally a place where remnants of the ashes of the Buddha were buried; they have become places of pilgrimage for Buddhists. |
| | Sunday | The first day of the week; the Christian holy day since the fourth century. |
| | Synagogue | The Jewish place of worship. |
| **T** | Tallit | The Jewish prayer shawl; a four-cornered garment with fringes. |
| | Tefillin | Small leather boxes containing passages from the Torah, strapped on a Jewish man's arm and forehead for morning prayers on weekdays. |
| | Ten Commandments | The ten laws which Jews believe were given to Moses by God on Mount Sinai; known by Jews as the Ten Sayings. |
| | Theravada Buddhistm | One of the two main schools of Buddhism. |
| | Torah | 'Law' or 'teaching'; the first five books of the Jewish scriptures. |
| | Trimurti | Three important Hindu gods: Brahma, Vishnu and Shiva. |
| | Trinity | The Christian belief in God the Father, God the Son and God the Holy Spirit. |
| | Turban | The head-covering expected to be worn by Sikh men. |
| **V** | Virgin Mary | Mary, the mother of Jesus; called the Virgin Mary by Roman Catholics who address prayers to her. |
| | Vishnu | One of the most important Hindu gods. |
| **Y** | Yoga | 'Communion'; a way of uniting the soul with God through self-discipline. |